SPIRITUAL BASICS

Basic Biblical Keys For
Living A Spiritual Life

G. Michael Cocoris

© 2025 G. Michael Cocoris

All rights reserved. This publication may not be reproduced (in whole or in part, edited, or revised) in any way, form, or means, including, but not limited to electronic, mechanical, photocopying, recording or any kind of storage and retrieval system for sale, except for brief quotations in printed reviews, without the written permission of G. Michael Cocoris, 2016 Euclid #20, Santa Monica, CA 90405, michaelcocoris@gmail.com, or his appointed representatives. Permission is hereby granted, however, for reproduction of the whole or parts of the whole without changing the content in any way for free distribution, provided all copies contain this copyright notice in its entirety. Permission is also granted to charge for the cost of copying.

Unless otherwise indicated, all Scripture quotations are taken from the New King James Version ®, Copyright © 1979, 1980, 1982 by Thomas Nelson, Inc. Used by permission. All rights reserved.

Cover design by Mike and John Cocoris
Interior design by John Cocoris

Dedicated to Joshua Marshall,
a servant of Christ with the heart of a man of God,
and a desire to be a lean, mean Bible machine

TABLE OF CONTENTS

Introduction

Chapter 1 Spiritual Basics: Salvation   1

Chapter 2 Spiritual Basics: Assurance   13

Chapter 3 Spiritual Basics: Eternal Security   25

Chapter 4 Spiritual Basics: Trials   39

Chapter 5 Spiritual Basics: The Word of God   51

Chapter 6 Spiritual Basics: Understanding The Bible   65

Chapter 7 Spiritual Basics: Prayer   79

Chapter 8 Spiritual Basics: Growth   93

Chapter 9 Spiritual Basics: The Will of God   109

Chapter 10 Spiritual Basics: The Provision of God   141

Chapter 11 Spiritual Basics: The Love of God   153

Chapter 12 Spiritual Basics: The Judgement Seat   165

Conclusion   179

Bibliopraphy   181

About The Author   185

INTRODUCTION

It is not unusual for a Christian to be confused concerning basic biblical truths needed for spiritual growth. For example, in over 60 years of ministry, I have talked to hundreds of people who are confused about salvation. What must a person do to be saved? Some preachers say it is doing nothing more than praying a prayer, such as asking Jesus to come into your heart. Others claimed more is involved than praying a prayer. It is giving your life to Christ. Still, others proclaim that the condition of salvation is turning from sin and making Jesus the Lord of your life. No wonder there is confusion among Christians concerning something as simple as salvation.

Take another example. Many Christians are confused concerning the issue of assurance. Again, for more than six decades, I've talked to people who were not sure they were saved. I've had people tell me that they have asked Jesus to come into their hearts dozens of times, and they are still not sure they're going to heaven.

These two examples are only the beginning. To that short list could be added such things as confusion over eternal security, how to grow to spiritual maturity, and how to know the will of God, etc. Confusion over these issues produces spiritual instability. Paul says, "we all" need to come to the "knowledge of the Son of God, to the perfect man, to the measure of the stature of the fullness of

Christ that we should no longer be children, tossed two and fro and carried about by every wind of doctrine, by the trickery of men, in cunning craftiness of deceitful plotting" (Eph. 4:13-14). In other words, spiritually immature believers, here called "children," are "tossed two and fro and carried about by every wind of doctrine." In short, they are unstable spiritually.

Alongside spiritual instability is spiritual deception. Even older Christians can be deceived over some basic biblical truths needed to grow to spiritual maturity. For example, they think they know how to determine the will of God, but from a biblical point of view, they are mistaken and deceived.

So, what is the solution to confusion and deception that causes spiritual immaturity and instability? One way to answer that question is to get back to the basics. One definition of "back to basics" is "stressing simplicity and adherence to fundamental principles." We don't need complicated details or new theories. We need to concentrate on essential biblical truths necessary for spiritual growth.

Back to the basics in education emphasizes basic subjects such as reading, writing, and arithmetic, as well as grammar, history, and science. Back to the basics of health: getting enough sleep, exercise, and a healthy diet. The basic necessities of life are water, food, clothing, and shelter. The basic biblical truths needed for spiritual growth include salvation, assurance, eternal security, etc.

The material in this volume covers twelve basic biblical keys for living a biblical spiritual life. Since there is confusion and deception concerning some of these truths, those erroneous concepts will be exposed before the biblical perception is explained.

Chapter 1

SPIRITUAL BASICS: SALVATION

In just about everything we do, we have to learn the basics. For example, if you want to drive a car, you have to know such basic things as how to start it, how to put it in gear, what you must do to get it going, and what you must do to get it to stop. That's only the beginning. You must also learn about turn signals, windshield wipers, etc.

The same thing is true concerning living a spiritual life. To do that, you must learn some basic spiritual truths. In the case of living a spiritual life, however, there is a complication. Paul says, "And He Himself gave some *to be* apostles, some prophets, some evangelists, and some pastors and teachers, for the equipping of the saints for the work of ministry, for the edifying of the body of Christ, till we all come to the unity of the faith and of the knowledge of the Son of God, to a perfect man, to the measure of the stature of the fullness of Christ; that we should no longer be children, tossed to and fro and carried about with every wind of doctrine, by the trickery of men, in the cunning craftiness of deceitful plotting, but, speaking the truth in love, may grow up in all things into Him who is the head—Christ" (Eph. 4:12-15).

Gifted people, such as a pastor/teacher, equip saints for the work of the ministry so that as saints minister to one another, they become spiritually mature. Spiritual maturity is being Christlike, which is speaking the truth in love. But there is a complication. Instead of being spiritually mature, it's possible to be spiritually immature, tossed to and fro by every wind of teaching. Immature believers are tossed to and fro as if they were human tumbleweeds.

How does that happen? According to this passage, they have been listening to "every wind of doctrine," meaning listening to teaching that causes instability. In other words, it's possible to listen to and learn wrong teachings that produce immaturity instead of listening to correct biblical teachings that lead to spiritual maturity. Because of false teaching, there is confusion. We need to get back to basic spiritual truth.

We need to do this for two reasons. The first is education. Some do not know basic spiritual truths. The second reason for doing this is edification. We who know the spiritual basics need to understand how to communicate them when ministering to others.

Let's start with the subject of salvation. What must a person do to be saved?

Confusion: Popular Misconceptions

Give your life to Christ In the first place, the expression "Give your life to Christ, is not in the Scripture. In the second place, giving your life to Christ to be saved is backward. Christ gave His life for you. Jesus said He came to give His life a ransom for many (Mk. 10:45). Salvation is not based on what we do but on what Christ did.

Ask Jesus to come into your heart. Does not Revelation 3:20 say, "Behold, I stand at the door and knock. If anyone hears My voice and opens the door, I will come in to him and dine with him, and he with Me?" This is not a salvation verse written to those who don't know the Lord. This verse was written to Christians. Verse 19 says, "As many as I love, I rebuke and chasten. Therefore, be zealous and repent." The Greek word translated "chasten" means "child train." Verse 20 does not say he will come to save but to dine. The issue is fellowship, not salvation. The verse is not talking about Jesus coming into a person. It says He will come in to (two separate words), not into. Salvation is not based on what we do but on what Christ did.

Making Jesus Lord Does not Romans 10:9 say, "If you confess with your mouth the Lord Jesus and believe in your heart that God has raised Him from the dead, you will be saved?" (See also ESV.) The NASB 2020 renders this verse, "If you confess with your mouth Jesus as Lord." The NIV translates it, "If you declare with your mouth, 'Jesus is Lord.'" Both translations are incorrect. The words "as" and "is" are not in the Greek text.

The Greek word translated "Lord" has two basic meanings. In general, it is simply a title of respect given to a teacher. It's also used as a "divine title" (Abbott-Smith, p. 261). In the Old Testament, the sacred name of God was Yahweh. The Jews didn't want to pronounce that sacred name, so they said Adonai, the Hebrew word for Lord. The title "the Lord Jesus Christ means that Jesus is God (Lord) and Messiah ("Christ" is the Greek word for Messiah").

The real issue in Romans 10:9 is the meaning of "saved." In the New Testament, "save" can mean: I have been saved (past tense), I am being saved (present tense), or I will be saved (future tense). I have been saved from the penalty of sin. I am being saved from the power of sin. I will be saved from the presence of sin.

In Romans, "saved" is what happens *after* justification. "Much more then, having now been justified by His blood, we shall be saved from wrath through Him. For if when we were enemies we were reconciled to God through the death of His Son, much more, having been reconciled, we shall be saved by His life" (Rom. 5:9-10). "Save" in Romans 10:9 is what happens after justification. Romans 10:10 says, "For with the heart one believes unto righteousness, and with the mouth, confession is made unto salvation." In other words, in Romans, "saved" is being saved from the power of sin. Salvation from the penalty of sin is based on what Christ did, not what we do. Salvation from the power of sin is based on Christ's life in us and our dependence on Him.

Become a Disciple Some say one must become a disciple to be saved, but listen to what Jesus said about becoming a disciple. "If anyone comes to Me and does not hate his father and mother, wife and children, brothers and sisters, yes, and his own life also, he cannot be My disciple. And whoever does not bear his cross and come after Me cannot be My disciple. For which of you, intending to build a tower, does not sit down first and **count the cost**, whether he has *enough* to finish *it*—lest, after he has laid the foundation, and is not able to finish, all who see *it* begin to mock him, saying, 'This man began to build and was not able to finish'" (Lk. 14:26-30; bold type added). Note: discipleship costs.

Salvation is free. Romans 3:24 says, "Being justified freely by His grace through the redemption that is in Christ Jesus." Romans 6:23 says: "The gift of God is eternal life." Revelation 22:17 says, "The Spirit and the bride say, 'Come!' and let him who hears say, 'Come!' and let him who thirsts come. Whoever desires, let him take the water of life freely" (Rev. 22:17). Salvation is free; it is without cost! Salvation is not based on what we do but on what Christ did. Discipleship costs.

Other terminology used to say what one must do to be saved includes "give your heart to the Lord, turn from sin, be willing to turn from sin, etc." All such terminology is not biblical.

Clarification: The Biblical Teaching

Gospel of John The Gospel of John is the only book whose purpose is to tell us how to have eternal life. It says, "And truly Jesus did many other signs in the presence of His disciples, which are not written in this book; but these are written that you may believe that Jesus is the Christ, the Son of God, and that believing you may have life in His name" (Jn. 20:30-31). What does it mean to believe that Jesus is the Christ? Jesus answers that question in Luke 24, where He said, "And He opened their understanding, that they might comprehend the Scriptures. Then, He said to them, 'Thus it is written, and thus it was necessary for the Christ to suffer and to rise from the dead the third day'" (Lk. 24:45-46). Believing that Jesus is Christ means believing He died for sin and rose from the dead. That is the purpose of the gospel of John.

When Jesus told Nicodemus that he had to be born again, Nicodemus asked how. Jesus answered, "No one has ascended to heaven but He who came down from heaven, *that is,* the Son of Man who is in heaven. And as Moses lifted up the serpent in the wilderness, even so must the Son of Man be lifted up, that whoever believes in Him should not perish but have eternal life" (Jn. 3:13-15). In other words, Jesus told Nicodemus he had to believe that Jesus would die (Jn. 3:14) and He would be in heaven (Jn. 3:14), meaning He would be resurrected.

The Gospel of John was written as a unit. You cannot read the Gospel of John without concluding that Jesus died for sin (Jn. 1:29) and rose from the dead.

The Book of Romans The book of Romans contains the most detailed description of salvation of any book in the Bible. The first three chapters of Romans teach that all have sinned (Rom. 3:23). Then it says Christ was the propitiation for sin "by His blood" (Rom. 3:25). It speaks of His resurrection (Rom. 10:9). In Romans, the one place where it tells you how to be saved is chapter 4. It says, "But to him who does not work but believes on Him who justifies the ungodly, his faith is accounted for righteousness" (Rom. 4:5).

The Book of Galatians The book of Galatians is the one book written to refute the false view of what it takes to be saved. It says, "O foolish Galatians! Who has bewitched you that you should not obey the truth, before whose eyes Jesus Christ was clearly portrayed among you as crucified" (Gal. 3:1). Paul says, "Christ lives in me" (Gal. 2:20), recognizing the resurrection of Jesus. Galatians declares, "For you are all sons of God through faith in Christ Jesus" (Gal. 3:26).

The Gospel of John, Romans, and Galatians all teach that salvation is by faith in the son of God who died for sin and rose from the dead.

Clarification: The Biblical Details

What has to be believed? As has been pointed out, the Gospel of John says one has to believe Jesus is the Christ, the Son of God, and that believing Jesus is the Christ means that He died for sin and rose from the dead. One way or another, Romans and Galatians say the same thing.

To say the same thing another way, Christ's death for sin and resurrection from the dead are called of the gospel (1 Cor. 15:3-5). In the Great Commission, Jesus said to proclaim the *gospel* (Mk. 16:15) and those who believed the *gospel* would be saved (Mk. 15:16). Peter got the point. In the book of Acts, he preached the death and resurrection of Jesus and said that the death and resurrection of Jesus proved He was Christ! (Acts 2:22-36, esp. 2:36; 3:12-26, esp. 3:18 and 3:26; 4:9; 5:29-32; 10:36-43). Peter says that the Gentiles heard the *gospel* and believed (Acts 15:7).

Paul did the same thing. Luke says, "Then Paul, as his custom was, went in to them, and for three Sabbaths reasoned with them from the Scriptures, explaining and demonstrating that the Christ had to suffer and rise again from the dead, and *saying*, 'This Jesus whom I preach to you is the Christ'" (Acts 17:2-3). Notice it was Paul's *custom* to preach the gospel, that is, the death and resurrection of Christ.

Paul said to the Corinthians, "It pleased God through the foolishness of the message preached to save those who believe" (1 Cor. 1:21) and he goes on to identify the message when He writes, "But we preach Christ crucified" (1 Cor.1:23). Paul told the Corinthians that they were saved by believing the gospel, that is, the good news that Jesus died for their sins and rose from the dead (1 Cor. 15:1-5). That means that Paul's message in evangelism included the death and resurrection of Christ. Paul wrote to the Galatians, "O foolish Galatians! Who has bewitched you that you should not obey the truth, before whose eyes Jesus Christ was clearly portrayed among you as crucified?" (Gal. 3:1). In other words, when he evangelized them, Paul preached Christ crucified to the Galatians. Paul reminded the Thessalonians that "our gospel did not come to you in word only, but also in power, and in the Holy Spirit, and in much assurance" (1 Thess. 1:5). He preached the gospel, the death and resurrection of Christ (1 Cor. 15:1-5), to the Thessalonians.

In *Evangelism: A Biblical Approach*, I wrote, "The object of faith in the New Testament is Jesus Christ. If you were to look up all the occurrences of 'believe' and 'faith' in the New Testament to see what a person must know about Christ, you would discover that a person must believe four things: (1) that Christ is God

(John 20:31) and yet (2) a real man (1 John 4:2); (3) that He is the one who died for sins (Rom. 3:25) and (4) rose from the dead (Rom. 10:9)." I concluded, "The object of faith is Jesus Christ, the God-Man, who died and rose. It is not just any 'Christ.' The object of faith must be the Christ who is offered in the gospel, the one revealed in Scripture" (Cocoris, *Evangelism: A Biblical Approach*, pp. 68-69).

What does it mean to believe? The Greek word translated "believe" means "believe in something, be convinced of something." When a preposition is added ("believe in"), it means "depend on, put one's trust in" (Arndt and Gingrich, p. 660). The Greek word translated "faith" means "that which causes trust and faith, trust, confidence" (Arndt and Gingrich, p. 662).

After pointing out that Paul uses the noun (faith) whereas John prefers the verb (believe) with no essential difference in meaning, Bromiley says, "The main sense of the word 'faith' in the NT is that of trust or reliance" (*ISBE*, vol. II, p. 270). Ryrie says, "*Trust* may be particularly appropriate today, for the words *believe* and *faith* sometimes seem to be watered down so that they convey little more than knowing facts" (Ryrie, *So Great Salvation*, p. 121). Some scholars claim that when the verb "believe" is followed by a preposition such as "in" (*eis* in Jn. 3:16), "on" (*epi* in Acts 16:31), or "in" (*en* in Mark 1:15), it expresses reliance or trust (Bromiley in *ISBE*, vol. II, p. 270; Erickson, p. 940). Zane Hodges states that faith "is not mere assent or mere trust, it is the intelligent perception, reception, and reliance on the truth, *as revealed in the gospel!*" (Hodges, *Absolutely Free*, p. 29, italics added).

Repentance Some will say, "What about repentance? Does the Bible not say one must repent?" The answer is "yes" (Acts 17:30). The question is, "What is the definition of 'repent?'" The Greek word translated "repent" (the verb) means "change one's mind" (Arndt and Gingrich, p. 511). In some passages, it means "feel remorse" (Arndt and Gingrich, p. 512). The Greek word translated "repentance" (the noun) means "a change of mind." In some passages, it means "remorse. turning about" (Arndt and Gingrich, p. 512).

The Greek word repent does not include any relationship to sin. It is like the word dozen. Dozen means twelve. Twelve what? On a farm, it means twelve eggs. At the bakery, it means twelve donuts. Also, remember that a word can have different meanings in different contexts. For example, the English word "trunk" can mean the front and elephant or the back end of the car. So the question is, "What does the word "repent" mean in the New Testament?

In the New Testament, repent does not mean "feeling remorse." Paul made a distinction between feeling sorry and repenting. He says "sorrow led to repentance" (1 Cor. 7:9) and "godly sorrow produces repentance" (1 Cor. 7:10). That does not mean that sorrow always precedes repentance because Paul said, "The goodness of God leads you to repentance" (Rom. 2:4).

In the New Testament, repent does not mean "to turn." Repenting and turning are two different things (Acts 26:20; Rev. 2:5). John the Baptist told people to repent and bring forth fruit fit for repentance (LK. 3:8), which means that repentance is the root and the change of behavior the fruit.

In the New Testament, "repent" means "to change your mind." If you think works get you to heaven, you need to change your mind. Repentance is from dead works (Heb. 6:1). If you think God is a man-made idol, you need to change your mind (Acts 17:25, 29, 30). Repentance is changing her mind about God (Acts 20:21). In Acts 2, Peter told people they needed to change their minds because they thought Christ was a common criminal instead of the Lord of glory (Acts 2:38). In Revelation, people blasphemed the name of God and "they did not repent and give im glory" (Rev. 16:9). Revelation also speaks of people who "did not repent of their murders or their sorceries or their sexual immorality or their thefts" (Rev. 9:21). They needed to change their minds about their need of forgiveness for sin.

The Gospel of John, the book written to tell people how to have eternal life, uses the word "believe" to tell people what they must do to obtain eternal life, but it does not mention the word repent once. Romans, the most detailed book in the Bible concerning salvation, does not mention "repent" in the one chapter where Paul tells people what they must do to be justified, that is, chapter 4. In the one and only place in Romans where repentance is mentioned, it is a virtual synonym for faith (Rom. 2:4). Galatians, the one book in the New Testament designed to defend the gospel, does not contain the word repent.

Clearly, the emphasis in the New Testament is on faith. If people have an erroneous idea of God (Acts 20:21), Jesus (Acts 2:38), or works (Heb. 6:1), they need to change their minds about those things and trust Jesus Christ.

Summary: Salvation is believing Jesus Christ, the Son of God, died for sin and rose from the dead and trusting Him to save you.

In the Gospel of John, the issue is having eternal life. In Romans and Galatians, it is justification by faith. In the book of Acts and the epistles, it is being saved.

One of the passages that says it clearly is Ephesians 2:8-9. "For by grace you have been saved through faith, and that not of yourselves; *it is* the gift of God, not of works, lest anyone should boast" (Eph. 2:8-9). Also, see "But to him who does not work but believes on Him who justifies the ungodly, his faith is accounted for righteousness" (Rom. 4:5).

On a blank page in the back of your Bible, at the top of the page, write the word "Basics." Under that heading, write "1. Salvation," and after it, write "Ephesians 2:8-9."

When I talk to somebody and want to see if they understand the New Testament message about salvation, I ask them a question. When you stand before God and God asks you, "Why should I let you into my heaven?" what will you say? I want to hear them say something like, "I believe in Jesus" or "I believe Jesus died for me." But even if they give me that answer, I ask another question. Is that all you have? I want to hear them say, "Yes." Salvation is trusting Jesus Christ to get you to heaven. It is nothing more; it is nothing less!

Chapter 2

SPIRITUAL BASICS: ASSURANCE

Out of curiosity, I asked a professional counselor, "What is the most common problem you've seen in your practice?" She responded, "Anxiety and/or depression." There was a time in my life that if someone had asked me that question, I would've said, "The assurance of salvation." Perhaps it was because, at the time, I was an evangelist. So, it would have been natural for people to come to me with that problem. That is not the most common problem I see as a pastor, but it is a widespread problem among Christians. Many believers struggle with the assurance of salvation.

It is essential to get that issue settled because it's one of the basic spiritual truths you need to live a spiritual life. So, we need to ask and answer the question, "What does the Bible say about the assurance of salvation?

Some reading this will think, "I have assurance." I'm sure that's true, but there is no doubt that others do not. They need to know what the Scripture says about the assurance of salvation. But those who do have assurance need to know what the Bible says about this subject because they need to know how to help others that don't have assurance.

Confusion: Popular Misconceptions

Preachers What causes people to be confused about being sure they are saved? One cause of confusion is the preaching of some preachers. Not all preachers clearly understand even some of the most basic spiritual truths.

"Now a certain Jew named Apollos, born at Alexandria, an eloquent man *and* mighty in the Scriptures, came to Ephesus. This man had been instructed in the way of the Lord, and being fervent in spirit, he spoke and taught accurately the things of the Lord, though he knew only the baptism of John. So, he began to speak boldly in the synagogue. When Aquila and Priscilla heard him, they took him aside and explained to him the way of God more accurately. And when he desired to cross to Achaia, the brethren wrote, exhorting the disciples to receive him; and when he arrived, he greatly helped those who had believed through grace; for he vigorously refuted the Jews publicly, showing from the Scriptures that Jesus is the Christ" (Acts 18:24-38)

Notice Apollos was eloquent, mighty in the Scripture, instructed in the way of the Lord, and fervent in spirit. In his case, he wasn't preaching anything necessarily wrong. It was that there were things he did not know. So, Aquila and Priscilla privately explained to him the way of God more accurately. Today, some preachers need to be instructed in the way of the Lord more accurately.

James 2 For example, some preachers teach that even though you have faith, you might not have saving faith. According to them, there is a false faith. Based on the statement, "Faith without works is dead" (Jas. 2:17), they claim that if you do not have works, you do not have genuine faith. James 2 does not teach that if you do not have works, you do not have genuine faith. To correctly understand that passage, you must look at it in its context.

The context is the Judgment Seat of Christ (Jas. 2:12-13). James says faith without works cannot save you from being judged at the Judgment Seat of Christ (Jas. 2:14).

Although "If someone says he has faith" (Jas. 2:14) sounds like the person does not have real faith, the following statement indicates his faith is genuine. It says, "Can faith save him?" (Jas. 2:14). Dead faith does not mean the faith is nonexistent. It means it's inactive. To say that the battery in my car is dead doesn't mean it's nonexistent; it means it needs to be charged.

The Greek word translated "save" appears five times in James. None of them referred to being saved to go to heaven. For example, James says, "The prayer of faith shall save the sick" (Jas. 5:15). The issue in James 2 is profit (Jas. 2:14), that is, profit at the Judgment Seat of Christ. To profit at the Judgment Seat of Christ, believers must do things such as give food and clothing to those in need (Jas. 2:15-17).

At this point in the passage, James introduces an objector (Jas. 2:18-20). The objector seems to say there's no connection between faith and works. James calls such a person a "foolish man (Jas. 2:20). James demonstrates the connection by saying that

Abraham was justified by faith (Jas. 2:23). Years later, when he offered Isaac his "faith was working together with his works and by works faith was made perfect" (Jas. 2:22.

In other words, this passage teaches that genuine faith must have works to be profitable at the Judgment Seat of Christ and produce maturity in this life. Does that mean that the believer might not have works? Paul contemplates the possibility of a believer standing before the Judgment Seat of Christ with no works. Yet he is saved "so as through fire" (1 Cor. 3:11-15).

1 John Some preachers contend that 1 John contains tests of faith. Some say 1 John gives three tests. Christians can know they have authentic faith if they 1) believe Jesus is the Son of God, 2) obey His commands, and 3) love others. Others say there are nine tests: 1) walking in the light (1 Jn. 1:5-7), 2) confession of sin (1 Jn. 1:8-10), 3) obedience (1 Jn. 2:3-4), 4) love of the brethren (1 Jn. 2:9-11), 5) hatred of the world (1 Jn. 2:15-17), 6) perseverance and doctrine (1 Jn. 2:24-25), 7) righteousness (1 Jn. 3:10), 8) spirit's testimony (1 Jn. 4:13), 9) discipline (Heb. 12:5-8).

John did not write 1 John because he thought they needed a test to see if they were saved. He says, "I write to you, little children because your sins are forgiven you for His name's sake. I write to you, fathers because you have known Him *who is* from the beginning. I write to you, young men, because you have overcome the wicked one. I write to you, little children, because you have known the Father" (1 Jn 2:13-14).

A father asked me to talk to his son, who was in his 20s, concerning his salvation. When I met with the son, he said nine months before, he was sure he was saved. Then, he started attending a church where the pastor taught people had to pass tests to know if they were saved. He told me that after listening to that preaching for nine months, he was totally confused about the assurance of his salvation.

Clarification: The Possibility of Assurance

The Bible teaches you can *know* you have eternal life. John says, "These things I have written to you who believe in the name of the Son of God, that you may know that you have eternal life and that you may *continue to* believe in the name of the Son of God" (1 Jn. 5:13). Paul says, "I know whom I have believed and am persuaded that He is able to keep what I have committed to Him until that Day" (2 Tim. 1:12). It is not presumption to say that I know I have eternal life, that is, I know I am going to heaven.

"For our gospel did not come to you in word only, but also in power, and in the Holy Spirit and in much assurance, as you know what kind of men we were among you for your sake" (1 Thess. 1:5). "And we desire that each one of you show the same diligence to the full assurance of hope until the end" (Heb. 6:11). "Let us draw near with a true heart in full assurance of faith, having our hearts sprinkled from an evil conscience and our bodies washed with pure water" (Heb. 10:22). "The 'full assurance of faith' means unwavering confidence; a fulness of faith in God which leaves no room for doubt" (Barnes). "We draw near with utter confidence in the promises of God and with the firm conviction that we shall have a gracious reception into His presence" (MacDonald). "With no doubt as to our acceptance when coming to God by the blood of Christ" (JFB).

It is not only possible to know you are saved, but it is also possible to know that you are saved the *day* you are saved. Jesus told a parable about two men who went to the temple to pray (Lk. 18:10-13). The Pharisee thanked God that he was not "like other men; extortioners, unjust, adulterers, or even as this tax collector" (Lk. 18:11). The tax collector prayed, "God, be merciful to me a sinner!" (Lk. 18:13). Jesus says, "I tell you, this man went down to his house justified rather than the other." The implication is that the sinner went home knowing he was saved.

Another case is the thief on the cross. When the thief said, "Lord, remember me when You come into Your kingdom" (Lk. 23:42), "Jesus said to him, 'Assuredly, I say to you, today you will be with Me in Paradise'" (Lk. 23:43). There is no doubt that the thief on the cross knew he was saved—the day he was saved. Jesus told him so.

Clarification: The Basis of Assurance

The issue is *how* you know that you are saved. What is the basis of assurance? From a biblical point of view, assurance is based on Christ's work and God's Word.

The Death of Christ When Christ died on the cross for our sins, He did everything necessary for us to go to heaven. On the cross, He cried, "It is finished!" (Jn. 19:30). Our sin debt was paid in full.

We can be assured of eternal life because Jesus died for our sins.

In his book *Full Assurance*, Harry Ironside says our peace with God "rests not on me, not on the frames of my hand or experiences, but from the finished work of Christ and the testimony of the word of God" (Ironside, p. 8).

Referring to Isaiah 53, he writes, "'He was wounded for our transgressions.' Make it personal! Put yourself and your own sins in there. Read it as though it said, 'He was wounded for *my* transgressions.' Do not get lost in the crowd. If there had never been another sinner in the world, Jesus would have gone to the cross for you! Oh, believe it and enter into peace! 'He was bruised for our iniquities.' Make it personal! Think what your ungodliness and your self-will cost Him. He took the blows that should have fallen upon you. He stepped in between you and God as the rod of justice was about to fall. It bruised Him in your stead. Again, I plead, make it personal! Cry out in faith, 'He was bruised for *my* iniquities.' Now, go further. 'The chastisement of our peace was upon him.' All that was necessary to make peace with God He endured. 'He made peace through the blood *of* his cross.' Change the 'our' to 'my.' 'He made *my* peace'" (Ironside, p. 20).

The Nature of Faith To say the same thing another way, assurance comes with faith. The traditional translation of Hebrews 11:1 is "Faith is the substance of things hoped for, the evidence of things not seen" (KJV; NKJV), but other translations render Hebrews 11:1: "Now faith is assurance of things hoped for, a conviction of things not seen" (ASV), "Now faith is the assurance of *things* hoped for, the conviction of things not seen" (NASB). "Now faith is being sure of what we hope for and certain of what we do not see" (NIV). Faith is being sure; it is assurance.

John Calvin (1509-1564) teaches that faith includes assurance. He defines faith as "a firm and sure knowledge of the divine favor toward us, founded on the truth of a free promise in Christ and revealed to our minds, and sealed on our hearts, by the Holy Spirit" (Calvin, III, ii. 7). He calls faith a "full persuasion" of truth (Calvin, III. ii. 12) and speaks of being "firmly persuaded" (Calvin, III. ii. 6, II, ii. 16).

In his doctrinal dissertation at Oxford, later published under the title *Calvin and English Calvinism to 1649*, R. T. Kendall came up with a similar list of expressions Calvin used to describe faith (Kendall, p. 19). He lists words such as "illumination" (Calvin, III. i. 4), "certainty" (Calvin, III. ii. 6), "firm conviction" (Calvin, III. ii. 16), "assurance" (Calvin, III. ii. 16), "firm assurance" (Calvin, III. ii. 16), and "full assurance" (Calvin, III. ii. 22). In other words, John Calvin captures the concept that faith as being persuaded and assured. Assurance comes with faith.

As Machen says, "Faith means not doing something but receiving something; it means not the earning of a reward but the acceptance of a gift" (Machen, *What is Faith?* p. 195).

In *Systematic Theology*, Berkhof says that the reformers sometimes spoke as if "one who lacks the assurance of salvation did not possess true faith" (Berkhof, p. 507). He points out that the Heidelberg Catechism "conceives of the assurance of salvation is belonging to the essence of faith" (Berkhof, p. 507). Berkhof himself, a Reformed theologian, insists that faith includes an element of personal assurance (Berkhof, p. 505). When you have trusted Christ, you *know* you have trusted Christ. How could you trust Christ without knowing it? Furthermore, you trust Him for eternal life (1 Tim. 1:16).

The Statements of Scripture To be assured of eternal life, take God at His Word. God's Word says, "Whoever believes in Him should not perish but have eternal life" (Jn. 3:15). "He who believes in the Son has everlasting life; and he who does not believe the Son shall not see life, but the wrath of God abides on him" (Jn. 3:36). "He who has the Son has life; he who does not have the Son of God does not have life" (1 Jn. 5:12).

God promised that if you trust Christ, you will have eternal life. John wrote, "This is the promise that He has promised us—eternal life" (1 Jn. 2:25). It is believing God's promise, not making God a promise. God said it. I believe it. That settles it.

One Greek professor says faith is "the inward conviction that what God says to us in the gospel is true" (Hodges AF, p. 31) and faith is "taking God at His Word. Saving faith is taking God at His Word in the gospel. It is nothing less than this. But it is also nothing more" (Hodges, AF, p. 32).

Francis Schaeffer agrees, "The Bible makes it plain that the man who is a Christian has a right to know that he is saved: it is one of the good gifts of God, to know truly that he is a Christian. This refers not only to the initial fact after one has accepted Christ as Savior, it also applies to those great and crushing moments in our lives when the waves get so high that it seems, psychologically or spiritually, and we can never find our footing again. At such a moment, a Christian can have assurance. His salvation rests on the finished work of Christ whether he accepts the peace he should have or not, and he can have assurance to the extent to which he believes the promises of God at that moment" (Schaeffer, pp. 77-78).

Torrey says, "It is the blood of Christ that makes it safe; it is the word of God that makes it sure" (Torrey, pp. 480-481).

Some have a problem with the assurance of their salvation because they do not "feel" saved. When I talk to people with that problem, I ask, "Are you an American citizen?" When they respond in the affirmative, I asked, "How do you know you are an American citizen?" Do you feel that you are an American citizen right now?" The answer is we know that we are citizens because we have a birth certificate. Pointing that out, I tell them, "We base our American citizenship on a piece of paper!" In the same way, we base our heavenly citizenship on a piece of paper—the Word of God.

Summary: Because God said, "He who believes in the Son has everlasting life," those who trust Christ for eternal life can know they are going to heaven.

On a blank page in the back of your Bible, under the word "Basics," write "2. Assurance," and after that, write "John 3:36."

This issue comes down to whether you are trusting something you do to get to heaven or are you trusting Jesus Christ and what He did in dying on the cross for your sins and being raised from the dead. I have illustrated this using a whiteboard or an 8.5 x 11 piece of paper-turned landscape. I draw a horizontal line at the bottom of the board or the paper. On the left-hand side of that line, I draw a stick figure. Above and still further left of the stick figure, I draw a cross and an arrow from the stick figure to the cross. I explained that we look at Christ and His death on the cross and resurrection from the dead when we get saved. Then, I go to the right-hand side of the page about a horizontal line and draw another stick figure. I point out that when people doubt their salvation, they look at themselves. So, I draw an arrow from the stick figure on the right to the stick figure on the left. That's the problem. Those doubting their salvation look at themselves and not at Christ. The solution is to look to Christ and the cross. So, I draw an arrow from the stick figure on the right side of the page to the cross behind the stick figure on the left. Assurance comes from looking at Christ and what He did, not at ourselves.

Queen Victoria of England once heard a sermon that greatly impressed her. Later, she asked her chaplain, "Is it possible to be absolutely sure of this life of eternal safety?" He replied, "I know of no way that one could be absolutely sure." This incident was later published in the Court News, which came to the attention of a minister named John Townsend. As a result, he sent the following letter to the Queen: "To her gracious Majesty, our beloved Queen Victoria, from one of her most humble subjects. With trembling hands but love-filled heart, and because I know that we can be absolutely sure even now of our eternal life in the home Jesus went to prepare, I would ask you, Most Gracious Majesty, to read the following passages of Scripture: John 3:16; Romans 10:9, 10. These passages prove there is full assurance of salvation by faith in our Lord Jesus Christ for those who believe and accept His finished work."

Several days later, Townsend received this note: "Your letter of recent date received, and in reply, I would state that I have carefully and prayerfully read the portions of Scripture referred to. I believe in the finished work of Christ for me and trust by God's grace to meet you in that home of which He said, 'I go to prepare a place for you.'"

Chapter 3

SPIRITUAL BASICS: ETERNAL SECURITY

After preaching two messages in this series, I announced that the following message would be on eternal security. After the service, two people asked if I would address a particular situation. One was about people and the way they live. The other person had passages of Scripture in mind. People have questions about the possibility of believers losing their salvation. Is that possible?

Confusion: Popular Misconceptions

Galatians 5:4 One of the most often-used verses against the doctrine of eternal security is the one that speaks about falling from grace. In Galatians, Paul says, "You have become estranged from Christ, you who *attempt to* be justified by law; you have fallen from grace" (Gal. 5:4). People claim that Galatians 5:4 teaches believers can fall from grace into sin, meaning they lose their salvation.

Paul plainly says that *those who fall from grace are those who are attempting to be justified by the Mosaic Law*. To fall from grace, believers must fall into the trap of trying to keep the Law. Falling here is not into sin. It is falling into law-keeping. It is not falling into badness; it is falling into goodness. This verse is not talking about a lawbreaker; it is talking about a law-keeper!

On his first missionary journey, Paul came to Galatia, led people to Christ and established churches (Gal. 3:1-3). After his departure, the Judaizers told these new converts they had to keep the Law to be right with God. They began observing Jewish holy days (Gal. 4:10-11) and were contemplating being circumcised (Gal. 5:3).

Hence, the issue in the book of Galatians is law versus grace. Paul's point is if believers try to be righteous before God by using a law system, they have fallen from a grace system. The phrase translated, "You have become estranged from Christ," means "to make idle or inactive, to render inoperative." Believers trying to live by law to be righteous before God have rendered Christ inactive. They are working to keep the Law without Him.

It would be like believers today thinking they can obtain righteousness before God by going to church on Sunday, reading their Bible, and giving money. They have fallen from grace by trying to be acceptable to God by performance. Believers can fall from living by grace, but they cannot fall from salvation.

Turning from the principle of grace to legalism to gain favor with God is falling from grace, not falling from salvation. They have fallen from grace in that they do not depend on the grace of God; they depend on law-keeping.

Galatians 5:19-24 Those who teach that you can lose your salvation often use verses that speak about not inheriting the kingdom of God. For example, Paul says, "Now the works of the flesh are evident, which are: adultery, fornication, uncleanness, lewdness, idolatry, sorcery, hatred, contentions, jealousies, outbursts of wrath, selfish ambitions, dissensions, heresies, envy, murders, drunkenness, revelries, and the like; of which I tell you beforehand, just as I also told *you* in time past, that those who practice such things will not inherit the kingdom of God" (Gal. 5:19-21). Other passages speak of not inheriting the kingdom of God (1 Cor. 6:9-10; Eph. 5:5). The passages on not inheriting the kingdom are used to either teach that people committing such sins were never saved in the first place or people who commit such sins lose their salvation.

Look at the context. Paul says, "Walk in the Spirit and you will not fulfill the lust of the flesh" (Gal. 5:16). That verse definitely talks about believers. The subject of this passage is believers either walking in the Spirit or the lust of the flesh. Then Paul lists the works of the flesh (Gal. 5:19-21). Can believers commit the sins listed in Galatians 5:19-21? Of course. Notice that jealousy, envy, and contentions are listed side by side with idolatry, adultery, and murder. If believers can commit such sins, does that mean they were never saved, or they were saved and lost their salvation?

The issue is what the Bible teaches about inheritance. In the Old Testament, all Israelites received land in Canaan as an inheritance (Deut. 19:14; 25:19; 26:1; Ps. 105:10-11). Some Israelites received a double inheritance (Deut. 21:15-17). Some were disinherited. In Genesis 49, Jacob gave his sons their inheritance. One received a double portion (Joseph) and three were disinherited (Reuben, Simeon, and Levi).

For example, as the firstborn son, Reuben should have been given preeminence among his brothers, leadership of the tribes, priesthood within the family, and a double portion of his birthright (Deut. 21:17), but because of his sexual immorality with Bilhah, his father's concubine (Gen. 35:22), he was disinherited (1 Chron. 5:1-2). Jacob told him he was "unstable as water" and would "not excel" because he "defiled his father's bed" (Gen. 49:4). Neither Reuben nor his descendants ever excelled. The leadership of the tribes went to Judah, the priesthood to Levi (**Exod. 32:25-29; Num. 3:12-13**), and the double portion to Joseph. Reuben lost his right to an additional inheritance other than entering the land. Because of sexual immorality, fierce anger, and cruelty, these brothers were disinherited, but they were allowed to live in the Promised Land.

In other words, in the Old Testament, there is a difference between entering the land and inheritance. A simple illustration is the difference between entering and inheriting a house. In the New Testament, to enter the kingdom, one must be born again (Jn. 3:5). To inherit the Kingdom is to rule and reign with Christ in it. To qualify for that, one must walk in the Spirit now and not fulfill the lust of the flesh to produce the works of the flesh (Gal. 5:16, 19-21).

There is a sense in which all who have trusted Christ are heirs (Gal. 3:29). Yet, there is another sense in which only those who faithfully follow the Lord and suffer with Him in the process will be joint-heirs with Christ in ruling over the Kingdom (Rom. 8:17). James 2:5 is referring to those who are rich in faith, become joint-heirs with Christ and rule and reign with Him in the Kingdom.

Matthew 24:13 In the Olivet discourse, Jesus said, "But he who endures to the end shall be saved" (Mt. 24:13; see also Mt. 10:22). This verse is often interpreted to mean those who persevere in their spiritual life will be saved spiritually, implying that those who do not persevere will not be saved. Does that mean that believers have to endure to make it to heaven?

To interpret any verse in the Bible, one must first ask, *"What is the subject being discussed?"* That is true of any ordinary conversation. Imagine that members of a family were sitting at the kitchen table discussing whether to go to a particular movie. Everyone decides to go. At that point, one of the daughters leaves the room. While she is gone, the conversation changes to what to wear. The mother asks her son, "Are you going to wear your blue shirt?" As he answers, his sister reenters the room just in time to hear him say, "No, I don't think I will." She then turns to her brother and says, "Why are you not going with us?" She misunderstood his answer because she was unaware that the subject being discussed had changed.

What is the subject of Matthew 24? The passage begins, "Now as He sat on the Mount of Olives, the disciples came to Him privately, saying, 'Tell us, when will these things be? And what *will be* the sign of Your coming, and of the end of the age?'" (Mt. 24:3). In answering that question, Jesus describes the Tribulation, which takes place just before His coming (Mt. 24:21, 29). In other words, *the subject of Matthew 24:4-29 is the Tribulation.*

So, in this passage, the apostles asked about the end of the *age* (Mt. 24:3). In answering their question, Jesus mentions "the end" three times (Mt. 24:6, 13, 14). In each case, the end is not the end of one's life but the end of the Tribulation.

In this passage, endurance is enduring the persecution of the Tribulation (Mt. 24:9-12). It is enduring arrest, scourging, trials before religious and civic leaders, as well as rejection by one's own family.

The Greek word translated "saved" means "save, deliver." In this passage, "saved" is not salvation from sin but deliverance from physical death. Jesus says, "And unless those days were shortened, no flesh would be saved; but for the elect's sake those days will be shortened" (Mt. 24:22). No flesh being saved means no one escapes physical death.

In the middle of a discussion on the Tribulation, Jesus says, "He who endures to the end (of the Tribulation) shall be saved" (delivered from physical death) (Mt. 24:22). This passage has nothing to do with eternal security. That is not the subject being discussed.

John 15:6 In the upper room discourse, Jesus said, "If anyone does not abide in Me, he is cast out as a branch and is withered; and they gather them and throw *them* into the fire, and they are burned" (Jn. 15:6). Some say this verse means that if believers do not abide, they will end up in hell.

The *subject* of this passage is *fruit bearing*. Jesus speaks of believers having no fruit (Jn. 15:2), fruit (Jn. 15:2), more fruit (Jn. 15:2), and much fruit (Jn. 15:5). The point is that if believers abide in Christ, they will produce more and more fruit.

In the middle of discussing fruit, Jesus says those who do not abide will be cast into a fire. Some say this is not referring to genuine believers, but Jesus says He is talking about "every branch in Me" (Jn. 15:2). He told the disciples, "You are the branches" (Jn. 15:5). Those cast forth are cast forth as branches (Jn. 15:6). This passage is talking about non-abiding, unfruitful believers. The problem is that these believers do not abide in Christ and consequently are thrown into the fire.

The fire in this verse has sparked a bonfire of controversy. The question is, "Where and when is a believer cast forth as a Christian into the fire?" It is important to remember that the fire of hell is not the only fire mentioned in the Bible.

Some say the fire here is uselessness. Derickson and Radmacher say that the fire illustrates uselessness, not destruction (as does Haddon Robinson in a sermon on this passage). In fact, vine wood is worthless as wood. Furniture cannot be made from it, nor anything else.

The fire in this verse could be the fire of trials (1 Pet. 1:7; 4:12). Wiersbe says that the fire in this verse "describes divine discipline rather than eternal destiny."

This fire has also been explained as the fire at the Judgment Seat of Christ (Dillow). The objection to the suggestion that the fire in John 15:6 is the Judgment Seat of Christ is that the *branch* is said to be cast in the fire and not just his works, but believers at the Judgment Seat of Christ are saved "through fire" (1 Cor. 3:15).

In a sense, all three of these are true. Believers who do not abide are useless, will be disciplined, and will suffer loss at the

Judgment Seat of Christ. Jesus commands believers to abide to produce fruit. Not abiding means loss. It is either fruit or fire.

Serious Sin What about "major" sins? All sin is sin, but some are more serious than others. If believers commit serious sins, does that cause them to lose their salvation?

Paul says to the Corinthians, "It is actually reported that there is sexual immorality among you and such sexual immorality as is not even named among the Gentiles; that a man has his father's wife! And you are puffed up, and have not rather mourned, that he who has done this deed might be taken away from among you. I indeed, as absent in body but present in spirit, have already judged, as though I were present, concerning him who has so done this deed. In the name of our Lord Jesus Christ, when you are gathered together, along with my spirit, with the power of our Lord Jesus Christ, deliver such a one to Satan for the destruction of the flesh, that his spirit may be saved in the day of the Lord Jesus" (1 Cor. 5:1-5).

This believer was guilty of the gross sin of incest (1 Cor. 5:1). To make matters worse, this believer refused to repent (1 Cor. 5:2-3). Paul directed the church to deliver such a one to "Satan for the destruction of the flesh." The destruction of the flesh is physical death. In other words, this believer would have died in his sin (1 Cor. 11:30). Yet his spirit would be saved; he would go to heaven (1 Cor. 5:5).

This is conclusive proof of eternal security. This believer was living in open sin and refused to repent. That is why he is being disciplined. Paul contemplates his death *in sin* and yet says he will be saved at the Judgment Seat of Christ (1 Cor. 3:15). The fact that he did repent (2 Cor. 2:6) does not alter the point that Paul is teaching here that even if he died in sin without repentance, he would be saved.

Stop Believing Some argue that since salvation is by faith if believers cease to believe, they lose their salvation. They point out that in the Gospel of John, the word "believe" is very often in the present tense, indicating that believers must keep believing. They also claim that faith is the "condition" of salvation, and if someone ceases to meet it, they are lost again.

Must believers continue to believe to stay saved? Does the fact that "believe" is in the present tense in some passages mean that some believers do continue to believe or that all *must* continue to believe? The word "believe" also appears in the aorist tense (Acts 16:31), which describes a completed act. It is like dropping a coin off a bridge. Once done, it is done.

What does the Scripture say happens when a believer ceases to believe? Paul writes, "*This is* a faithful saying: For if we died with *Him,* We shall also live with *Him*. If we endure, we shall also reign with *Him*. If we deny *Him,* He also will deny us. If we are faithless, He remains faithful; He cannot deny Himself" (2 Tim. 2:11-13). This passage consists of four "if" clauses and a conclusion. Each "if" clause represents a choice. Each conclusion contains the consequences of that choice.

The first statement does not explicitly mention a choice, but one is implied, namely, faith in Christ. Paul is speaking about the death of the "old man" when people trust Christ (Rom. 6:1-6;

Gal. 2:20). The consequence of trusting Christ is being made spiritually alive with Christ.

The second statement concerns the choice of enduring suffering for Christ's sake. The consequence is reigning with Christ in His future kingdom (Rom. 8:17).

The third statement is about the choice of denying Him. This is a believers' denial of the Lord (see "we," Paul includes himself; see Lk. 22:54-62, esp. 22:61). The consequence of believers denying the Lord is the Lord will deny them.

So what is denied believers who deny the Lord? The Greek word translated "deny" in 2 Timothy 2:12 is the same one rendered "deny" in Matthew 10:32. Both Paul and Jesus are talking about *believers* (remember "we") denying (disowning) the Lord before men (remember Peter). This means that Jesus will deny believers before the Father (Mt. 10:32-33). When believers disown the Lord, they are denied *reward* before the Father (Mt. 10:41-42). The issue is not faith versus denial of faith. It is the public confession of Christ versus the public disowning of Christ. The consequence of publicly disowning Christ is a denial of reward.

The fourth statement is about the choice of ceasing to believe. The Greek word translated "faithless" means "to disbelieve, be faithless." In *The King James Version*, it is translated "if we believe not." The consequence is that even if believers cease to believe, God remains faithful to His promise. "He cannot deny Himself." The believer's greatest security is the Lord's faithfulness to His own promise (Guthrie).

Believers cannot lose their salvation by a lack of works, sinning, or unbelief.

Clarification: Guarantee of Salvation

The Provision of Jesus For clarification, let's start with the nature of the transaction called salvation. What is it that Jesus provides to those who believe? "He who believes in the Son has everlasting life and he who does not believe the Son shall not see life, but the wrath of God abides on him" (Jn. 3:36). If you believe in the Son, what do you have? The answer is "eternal life." You do not have temporary life; you have eternal life. Dr. Charles Ryrie said, "If everlasting life could be lost, then it has the wrong name." Believers can lose the assurance of salvation by taking their eyes off the promise; they cannot lose salvation itself because it is *eternal* life. Furthermore, this provision of Jesus is a gift (Rom. 6:23) and God never changes His mind about giving a gift. His gifts are irrevocable (Rom. 11:29).

The Prayer of Jesus An often-overlooked teaching of the New Testament is that Jesus Christ is praying for believers. Hebrews says, "But He because He continues forever, has an unchangeable priesthood. Therefore, He is also able to save to the uttermost those who come to God through Him since He always lives to make intercession for them" (Heb. 7:24-25). Jesus Christ is an unchanging and unchangeable High Priest praying for believers. Therefore, He can save them to the uttermost, that is, completely, totally.

For what does Jesus pray? While He was still on the earth, He said to God the Father, "I do not pray that You should take them out of the world, but that You should keep them from the evil one" (Jn. 17:15). Did Jesus ever have an unanswered prayer? If He did not, believers are guaranteed to be kept from Satan.

Therefore, believers are eternally secure because of Christ's prayer for them.

The Promise of Jesus Jesus said, "I give them eternal life, and they shall never perish; neither shall anyone snatch them out of My hand. My Father, who has given *them* to Me, is greater than all; and no one is able to snatch *them* out of My Father's hand" (Jn. 10:28-29). The Greek text "They shall never perish" contains a double negative plus the phrase "forever." This is one of the most emphatic statements in the New Testament, Which means that believers "shall certainly not perish forever." To reinforce that no one will be able to snatch the sheep from His hand, He adds the Father is greater than all and no one can snatch them from His hand.

The point is that believers are secure. It is as if the believer is in Christ and Christ is in the Father's hand. It is like money being in the safe, the safe being in the building, and an army is guarding the building.

Some say a believer can jump out of His hand. That cannot happen. Believers are not holding onto Jesus. Jesus is holding the believers, the Father is holding them, and He is greater than all, including you. The issue is not the perseverance of the saints; instead, it is the perseverance of God!

Solomon says, "Answer a fool according to his folly, lest he be wise in his own eyes" (Prov. 26:2). Here is an answer to a fool according to his folly: according to the New Testament, believers are part of His body; a finger cannot jump out of the hand.

In some parts of the mission field, the natives divide Christians into two classes. Some, they say, believe in "monkey religion." Monkeys carry their young by having the little ones hold on to the mother's tail. If the baby monkey is healthy and well, there is little danger, but if the small one, through sickness or weakness, loses his hold when the mother suddenly leaps from one branch to another, the little creature falls off. Others believe in "cat religion." A mother cat takes hold of the baby kitten with her teeth. The babies safely depend on the hold of the mother cat, not upon their own ability. Believers are secure, not because they hold on to God, but because God holds on to them.

Jesus said, "Most assuredly, I say to you, he who hears My word and believes in Him who sent Me has everlasting life, and shall not come into judgment, but has passed from death into life" (Jn. 5:24). He emphatically states that those who believe have passed from death to life and "shall not come into judgment." Having passed from spiritual death to spiritual life, it is no longer possible for believers to come into a judgment that decides eternal life. Believers have eternal life now. Eternal life is settled once and for all! In the words of a professor who wrote a 936-page commentary on the Gospel of John, "To have eternal life now is to be secure throughout eternity" (Leon Morris).

Summary: Scripture does not teach that believers can lose their salvation; it teaches they are eternally secure based on the provision of the transaction itself, the prayers of Jesus, and the promise of Jesus.

On a blank page in the back of your Bible, under the word "Basics," write "3. Security," and after that, write "John 5:24."

The great objection is, "Believing in eternal security gives people a license to sin." Eternal security is not a license to sin. According to the New Testament, if believers sin, God disciplines them (1 Cor. 11:30). Eternal security does not give believers the freedom to sin but to serve. Not believing in eternal security runs the risk of people serving the Lord out of fear. Believing in eternal security frees believers to serve out of love.

The San Francisco Bay Bridge cost $77,000,000 and dozens of lives to build. During the construction of the first section of the bridge, no safety devices were used, with the result that twenty-three men fell to their deaths in the waters below. During the construction of the second great section, the greatest safety net in the world, costing $100,000, was installed. This gigantic net made of stout manila cordage saved the lives of at least ten men who fell to it without injury. In addition to that, according to *The Readers' Digest*, "The work has gone fifteen to twenty-five percent faster with the men relieved of the ruinous fear of falling." The knowledge that they were safe left the men free to devote their energies to the particular tasks at hand.

To be assured of eternal life is not a license to sin. It frees believers up "to devote their energies to the particular tasks at hand."

Chapter 4

SPIRITUAL BASICS: TRIALS

To live a spiritual life, you must first establish a relationship with the Lord. In this "Spiritual Basics" discussion, I have explained how to do that. (See the first three chapters on salvation, assurance, and eternal security.) A sure, secure relationship with Jesus Christ is the foundation of the spiritual life. Paul said, "For no other foundation can anyone lay than that which is laid, which is Jesus Christ" (1 Cor. 3:11). After establishing a foundation of a relationship with the Lord, how do you build on it? What's next in a spiritual life?

The Traditional Message

After leading people to Christ, we speak of "follow-up," meaning that there are certain things we tell people after we lead them to the Lord. In my book on evangelism (*Evangelism: A Biblical Approach*), I conclude with a chapter on that subject. In it, I gave what I would call the usual or traditional material given to a new convert. Here is what I said. "There are as many ways to follow up a new convert as there are denominations and parachurch organizations. Every successful evangelist develops a new approach, usually rehearsing an old method. One system takes the new babes in Christ through ten steps to maturity as if they will be spiritually mature by the time they finish the ten lessons. A more modest approach puts all the information in a small booklet and admits that it only contains the first steps for newborn believers. If reading is too much work, audio versions are available.

"What material should be covered in follow-up? Must a method always begin with the assurance of salvation? That certainly seems logical, but is it scriptural? Is that how the apostles started? What method should be employed: booklets, books, or a bag full of audio recordings?

"Before we follow up, we should follow through. Follow-through is what is done in the initial conversation after people trust Christ. Follow-up comes later once we are sure people have trusted the Lord.

"Follow-through consists of discussing five things. The first is assurance.... After discussing assurance, I talk about 'getting to know Him.' ... That is done by communication. You talk to Him and He talks to you. Spiritually, that is done through Bible reading and prayer.... Follow-through also includes telling new Christians to be baptized.... The fourth item in follow-through is telling people about church.... The fifth and final part of follow-through is to ask if the new Christian has any questions. New converts will either have none or will ask something very elementary."

There is certainly nothing wrong with that approach. Everything in it is biblical, but where in the Bible does it say they did that? For that matter, what did they do in the Bible?

The Biblical Message

The Great Commission After the resurrection and before the ascension, on more than one occasion, the Lord gave the disciples a commission called "The Great Commission." Those five occasions are recorded in Matthew 28:18-20, Mark 16:15-18, Luke 24:46-48, John 20:21-23, Acts 1:8. The summary of those five passages is: preach the gospel, baptize those who believe, and teach them.

The Book of Acts The book of Acts records what Peter and Paul did with that commission. For example, in Acts 2, Peter preached the gospel, told those who believed to be baptized, and those who were baptized "continued steadfastly in the apostle's doctrine and fellowship, in the breaking of bread and in prayers" (Acts 2:42). In other words, Peter preached the gospel, baptize converts, and started a church. That was the pattern throughout Acts. They led people to Christ, baptized them immediately (Acts 8:26-38; 9:29-32; 18:8), and formed the church, where they taught them.

The Epistles What did they teach them? If they continued in the apostle's doctrine, and the New Testament is what the apostles taught, it is safe to assume what they taught them is recorded in the New Testament. Where did they start? What is the first thing they taught them?

Evidently, James was the first to write one of the books of the New Testament. They were still meeting in synagogues ("assembly" in 2:2 is the Greek word "synagogue"). James was probably written in AD 45. It has been placed as early as AD 34 (Hodges). The subject of the book is trials (Jas. 1:2-3; 5:13). Years later, when

Peter wrote his first epistle, one of the first things he did was talk about trials (1 Pet. 1:6-7; 4:12-13). After dealing in detail with the subject of justification by faith, the first thing Paul discusses in the book of Romans is trials (Rom. 5:3-4).

Interesting! Three authors in the New Testament, who wrote 16 of the 27 books of the New Testament, began with the subject of trials. Perhaps this tells us that one of the first things believers need to know about is trials. Problems are part and parcel of life. The dream of a carefree life is just that. It is a dream. Why is life filled with trouble? How are we supposed to handle trouble, trials, and tribulations?

What You Need to Know about Trials

James "My brethren, count it all joy when you fall into various trials, knowing that the testing of your faith produces patience. But let patience have *its* perfect work, that you may be perfect and complete, lacking nothing" (Jas. 1:2-4). The book of James refers to financial pressure (Jas. 1:9, 27), oppression (Jas. 2:6), disputes (Jas. 4:1), injustice (Jas. 5:1-6), illness (Jas. 5:14), and death (Jas. 1:27). In other words trials consist of, money, relationships, and heath.

James tells believers what to do. First, they are to "count it all joy." This joy is a "calm delight." James says, "Make up your mind to consider this trial as something about which you will be glad." Second, they are to trust the Lord. James is talking about tested, approved faith, that is, genuine faith. When trials come, believers are to trust the Lord for grace (2 Cor. 12:7-10). Third, they are to endure. Approved, genuine faith produces patience, a Greek word that means "endure."

James tells believers why they should count it all joy, trust the Lord, and endure to be perfect The Greek word translated "perfect" means "reaching its end, finished, complete, mature." Endurance makes believers mature (fully developed) and complete (with all the parts). The Lord allows trials to come into their lives to either add something to them or develop something already in them. Trials are for training.

Later in the passage, James says, "Blessed *is* the man who endures temptation; for when he has been approved, he will receive the crown of life which the Lord has promised to those who love Him" (Jas. 1:12). The Greek word translated "temptation" means "temptation, trials." In this verse, it refers to trials; trials are endured, not temptation. If believers endure trials, they will receive a reward at the Judgment Seat of Christ. Trials are for a trophy.

James is saying, "When trials come, if you trust the Lord, you will endure, grow toward maturity now, and be rewarded later." In other words, trials are for your training and for a trophy.

Peter "In this you greatly rejoice, though now for a little while, if need be, you have been grieved by various trials that the genuineness of your faith, *being* much more precious than gold that perishes, though it is tested by fire, may be found to praise, honor, and glory at the revelation of Jesus Christ" (1 Pet. 1:6-7). The occasion of 1 Peter was the news of growing opposition and persecution of believers in Asia Minor (1 Pet. 1:6; 3:13-17; 4:12-19;

5:9-10). Hostility and superstition were mounting. These believers were being slandered and attacked because of their faith (1 Pet. 3:14-15). They were being hated because of their withdrawal from sinful practices. Apparently, there were also charges against them of disloyalty to the state (1 Pet. 2:13-17).

Peter tells believers what to do. First, they are to "greatly rejoice!" They are to be glad when they are sad (Adams). The Greek word rendered "greatly rejoice" denotes intense joy, "to exult, to be overjoyed." Second, they are to trust the Lord because their faith is being tested by fire. Gold is put through the fire to burn out the impurities. The impurity in our faith that the fire of trials burns out is confidence in ourselves (2 Cor. 1:8-9). Trials bring us to the end of ourselves. Trials force us to depend on the Lord. No matter who you are, no matter how intelligent, no matter how talented, no matter how much money you have, no matter how many contacts you have, there will always be a problem you cannot solve. God will see to it that you are never in a place where you cannot do without Him. Third, they are to endure. Peter does not explicitly mention the word endurance, but it is implied by what he says next.

Peter tells believers why they should greatly rejoice, trust the Lord, and endure. He speaks of "receiving the end of your faith—the salvation of your souls" (1 Pet. 1:9). The Greek word translated "salvation" means "deliverance." It is used in the New Testament of our past deliverance from the penalty of sin (see "have been saved" in Eph. 2:8), our present deliverance from the power of sin (see "being saved" in 1 Cor. 1:18), and our future deliverance from the presence of sin (see Christ will appear *for* our salvation in Heb. 9:28). The salvation spoken of in 1 Peter 1:9 is the present deliverance from the power of sin. The Greek word translated "souls" means "life." In other words, as we learn to trust the Lord more and more, we are delivered more and more from the power of sin; our *life* is being saved (for other passages on the salvation of the soul, that is life, see Mt. 16:24-27; Jn. 12:25; Jas, 1:21). In short, we are growing spiritually. Trials are for training.

The faith that is developed will be rewarded. The reward will be praise, honor, and glory at the Judgment Seat of Christ. Praise is the verbal recognition and approval that will be given. It will be the "well done, good and faithful servant" from the Lord Himself (Mt. 25:21; 1 Cor. 4:5). Honor is the position of distinction, the rank, which will be bestowed (Jn. 12:26). "Glory" means "opinion, reputation, brightness, splendor." Hence, glory is the reputation or splendor that will be enjoyed. Trials are for a trophy.

Peter and James are saying the same thing. When trials come, if you rejoice, trust the Lord, and endure, you will grow to maturity now and receive a reward at the Judgment Seat of Christ. Trials are for your training and a trophy.

Paul "Rejoice in hope of the glory of God. And not only *that*, but we also glory in tribulations, knowing that tribulation produces perseverance; and perseverance, character; and character, hope" (Rom. 5:2b-4). The Greek word translated "tribulations" means "pressure" and is used figuratively for distress, affliction, physical hardship, and suffering. Today, we would use the word "stress."

Life is filled with problems. Those difficulties often provoke complaints, griping, and even murmuring against God.

Paul tells believers what to do. First, they are to glory in tribulation. The Greek word translated "glory" in verse 3 is the same Greek word translated "rejoice" in verse 2. Believers can rejoice, glory, boast, in their present troubles and be jubilant in their future hope. Second, they are to trust the Lord. Paul does not explicitly mention faith, but given that he discussed the faith of Abraham in Romans 4 and what he says next, it is safe to say that Paul assumes faith is part of the process. Third, they are to endure. Paul says that "tribulation produces perseverance." The Greek word translated "perseverance" in Romans 5 is the same Greek word that is translated "endurance" in James 1. Technically, it is not correct that tribulation produces perseverance or endurance. As James points out, and Paul leaves out, when trials and tribulations come, faith produces endurance. Tribulation produces endurance when, in the words of Cranfield, "it is met by faith in God which receives it as God's fatherly discipline" (2 Cor. 4:16, 18; esp. Jas. 1:2-3, which says that the approved part of faith produces endurance). At any rate, Paul teaches that tribulation produces endurance.

Paul tells believers why they should rejoice, trust the Lord, and endure. He says endurance produces character. The Greek word translated "character" means "approvedness." As believers endure tribulation, they develop qualities and virtues approved by God. Endurance develops "approved character." To add "proven" to character is like adding "sterling" to "silver." Trials are for training.

Paul adds that character produces hope, a Greek word that means "expectation." Believers "rejoice in hope of the glory of God" (Rom. 5:2). Believers can now boast in the sure expectation of the glory of God. The phrase "the glory of God" can mean either the glory God possesses or the glory He gives others. According to Peter, this is the glory given to believers at the coming of Christ. Trials are for a trophy.\

Paul is saying, "When tribulations come, if you endure, you will end up with character now and be rewarded later." Trials are for your training and a trophy.

Summary: After establishing a sure, secure relationship with Jesus Christ, believers need to learn that when trials come, they should rejoice, trust the Lord, and endure to develop maturity now and be rewarded at the Judgment Seat of Christ. Trials are for your training and a trophy.

On a blank page in the back of your Bible, under the word "Basics," write "4. Trials," and after that, write "Jas. 1:2-4." James, Peter, and Paul are saying the same thing. Peter leaves out endurance and Paul leaves out mentioning faith, but all three say that when trials come, if we trust the Lord, we will grow toward maturity now and be rewarded later. Trials are for your training and a trophy.

James: trials → rejoice → faith → endure → maturity → crown of life
1 Peter: trials → rejoice → faith → (endure) → growth → glory
Romans: tribulation → rejoice → (faith) → endure → character → glory

All three put this concept at the beginning of their discussion of the spiritual life. James and Peter obviously put it first. It might not appear that Paul puts it first, but he does. The first four chapters of Romans deal with justification. When he begins to discuss the spiritual life, the first thing he deals with is trials.

If children have it easy, it makes them weak. Struggles make them strong physically, mentally, emotionally, and spiritually.

Author and radio commentator Paul Harvey wrote a letter to his grandchildren called "These Things I Wish For You:"

"We tried so hard to make things better for our kids that we made them worse. For my grandchildren, I'd like better. I'd really like for them to know about hand-me-down clothes and homemade ice cream and leftover meatloaf sandwiches. I really would. My cherished grandson, I hope you learn humility by being humiliated and that you learn honesty by being cheated. I hope you learn to make your bed and mow the lawn and wash the car. And I really hope nobody gives you a brand new car when you are sixteen. I hope you have a job by then. It will be good if at least one time you can see a baby calf born and your old dog put to sleep. I hope you get a black eye fighting for something you believe in. I hope you have to share a bedroom with your younger brother. And it's all right if you have to draw a line down the middle of the room, but when he wants to crawl under the covers with you because he's scared, I hope you let him. When you want to see a Disney movie and your little brother wants to tag along, I hope you'll let him. I hope you have to walk uphill to school with your friends and that you live in a town where you can do it safely.

"On rainy days when you have to catch a ride, I hope your driver doesn't have to drop you two blocks away, so you won't be seen riding with someone as uncool as your mom. If you want a slingshot, I hope your dad teaches you how to make one instead of buying one. I hope you learn to dig in the dirt and read books. When you learn to use those newfangled computers, I hope you also learn to add and subtract in your head. I hope you get razzed by your friends when you have your first crush on a girl, and when you talk back to your mother that you learn what Ivory soap tastes like. May you skin your knee climbing a mountain, burn your hand on a stove and stick your tongue on a frozen flagpole. I hope you get sick when someone blows cigar smoke in your face. I don't care if you try beer once, but I hope you don't like it. And if a friend offers you dope or a joint, I hope you realize he is not your friend. I sure hope you make time to sit on a porch with your grandpa and go fishing with your uncle. May you feel sorrow at a funeral and the joy of holidays. I hope your mother punishes you when you throw a baseball through a neighbor's window and that she hugs you and kisses you at Christmas time when you give her a plaster of Paris mold of your hand.

Spiritual Basics: Basic Biblical Keys For Living a Spiritual Life

"These things I wish for you—tough times and disappointment, hard work, and happiness. With more love than you can ever know,
Grandpa Harvey"

God the Father knows struggles make us stronger. So rejoice, trust God, and endure because the trials are for your training and a trophy.

Chapter 5

SPIRITUAL BASICS: THE WORD OF GOD

The Bible uses several expressions to describe our relationship with the Lord. Those who have a relationship with the Lord are called "believers" (Acts 5:14; 1 Tim. 4:12). They are said to be "saved" (Acts 16:31), "justified" (Rom. 3:24, 28), and "born again" (Jn. 3:7). Those who are "born again," meaning they are born again spiritually, are called "babes in Christ" (1 Cor. 3:1).

What is the first thing all babies must have? Answer: milk. That's true of physical babies and that's true of spiritual babies. Peter says, "As newborn babes, desire the pure milk of the word, that you may grow thereby" (1 Pet. 2:2). Believers are commanded to desire the Word so they may grow spiritually. Assuming you desire the Word, what do you do? A physical baby gets milk by being breastfed or from a bottle. How does a spiritual baby get the Word of God?

Listen to It

Old Testament Throughout the Bible, the Word of God was spoken, and people listened. Peter says Noah was "a preacher of righteousness" (2 Pet. 2:5). People in Noah's day listened to the

Word of God. The Lord spoke His Word to Moses and Moses spoke to the children of Israel (Ex. 20:22). Moses "took the Book of the Covenant and read in the hearing of the people" (Ex. 24:7). People in Moses' day listened to the Word of God. The book of the Law was not to depart out of Joshua's mouth (Josh. 1:8). People in Joshua's day listened to the Word of God. The prophets preached the Word of God. For example, Jonah preached to the people of Nineveh (Jonah 3:4). The people of Nineveh listened to the Word of God.

New Testament John the Baptist (Mt. 3:1), the apostles (Mt. 10:7), and Jesus (Mt. 4:17) preached, "The kingdom of heaven is at hand." In their day, people listen to the Word of God. On the day of Pentecost, Peter preached (Acts 2:14). On the day of Pentecost, People listened to the Word of God, and 3000 were saved (Acts 2:41). Acts 17:13 records that Paul preached the Word of God. People in Paul's day listened to the Word of God.

God gives the gift of pastor/teacher (Eph. 4:11). Believers are to listen to pastors to teach the Word of God. Paul told Timothy, "Till I come, give attention to reading, to exhortation, to doctrine," that is, teaching (1 Tim. 4:13). Believers are to listen to pastors reading the Word of God. The Bible emphasizes *hearing* the Word of God preached. For example, it says, "How then shall they call on Him in whom they have not believed? And how shall they believe in Him of whom they have not heard? And how shall they hear without a preacher?" (Rom. 10:14). People are to listen to the Word of God.

I have heard that when people are dying, various parts of the body begin to shut down and the last thing to go is the hearing. As they are dying, even though there in a sleeplike state, they can still hear. So, loved ones often talk to them, believing they hear them even though they can't respond. Is it possible that God designed it so the dying person could listen to the Word of God?

This is clear: God wants people to hear the Word of God. That means you should attend a church that reads and teaches the Word of God. You can listen to the Word of God on your phone by downloading a free app. Just type "Bible" in the App Store. That app should not be a substitute for church, but it can be a supplement to listening to the Word of God.

Read It

Joshua "And there, in the presence of the children of Israel, he wrote on the stones a copy of the Law of Moses which he had written" (Josh. 8:32). There is a question about how much of the law was written. Some suggest that Joshua wrote the Ten Commandments. (Woudstra). Others believe that what he wrote was the blessings and cursings of Deuteronomy 27 and 28 (Bush). The Jews believed that what was written was the 613 commandments of the Pentateuch (Woudstra). Still, others have concluded that it was the whole book of Deuteronomy.

Archeologists have discovered inscribed pillars from six to eight feet in height in the Middle East. Some of these inscriptions were three times the length of the book of Deuteronomy (Campbell).

Later in history, daily newspapers were chiseled in stone six feet high and three feet wide. Tourists today can see examples of such stone newspapers in the ruins of ancient Ephesus.

God wants everyone to have access to His Word. When there was no parchment or printing, God said His Word was to be chilled in stone so people could read it.

Jesus Jesus repeatedly said, "Have you not read?" "Have you not read in the law that on the Sabbath the priests in the temple profane the Sabbath, and are blameless?" (Mt. 12:5). "Have you not read that He who made *them* at the beginning 'made them male and female'" (Mt. 19:4). "Have you never read, 'out of the mouth of babes and nursing infants you have perfected praise'" (Mt. 21:16). "Have you never read in the Scriptures: 'the stone which the builders rejected has become the chief cornerstone. this was the lord's doing, and it is marvelous in our eyes' ?'" (Mt. 21:42). "But concerning the resurrection of the dead, have you not read what was spoken to you by God" (Mt. 22:31).

Suggestions Many suggest reading the Bible every year. Doing that all at once would take the average reader 74 hours and 28 minutes. You can also read the entire Bible in a year if you read four or five chapters a day. You can start in Genesis and read straight through, or plans available that mix up what chapters you read each day. Google it.

Many years ago, I suggested that people should set aside seven minutes daily to spend time with the Lord. I called it a "Divine Date." The seven minutes were divided into three parts: prayer, reading, and prayer.

The first prayer including asking God to give you insight as you read. Psalm 119:18 says, "Open my eyes that I may see wondrous things from Your law."

Then, I suggested reading one chapter and looking for five things: 1) A Sin to Forsake, 2) A Command to Obey, 3) A Promise to Claim, 4) A Quality to Add, or 5) A Concept to Remember. Another method is to look for two things. "All Scripture *is* given by inspiration of God, and *is* profitable for doctrine, for reproof, for correction, for instruction in righteousness" (2 Tim. 3:16). The Scripture is for two things that are positive (doctrine and instruction) and two things that are negative (reproof and correction). In other words, the Scripture tells us to eliminate vices and incorporate virtues. The last prayer is spending a few minutes praying for other people.

I have also suggested that people read one book of the Bible all the way through every day for 30 days. If you do that, I highly recommend you begin with Philippians.

Meditate on It

What Do you do after you have read the Word of God? I suspect most would say, "You do what it says." Granted, God wants us to obey His Word, but not so fast. There's something you need to do before obedience.

The Bible emphasizes meditation. The Lord told Joshua to meditate in the Law day and night (Josh. 1:8). The psalmist wrote that the blessed man meditates in the Law of the Lord day and night" (Ps. 1:2). David said he meditated on the Lord in the night watches (Ps. 63:6), on all His work (Ps. 77:12; 143:5), His Word (119:148), His precepts (Ps. 119:15. 119:78), and His statues (Ps. 119:48). Psalm 119:23 declares, "Your servant meditates on Your statutes. If meditation is that important, we must understand what it is and how to do it.

Definition Two Hebrew words are translated "meditate." One means "moan, growl, meditate, muse" (Jos. 1:8; Ps. 1:2; 63:6; 77:12; 143:5). It is to ponder, imagine, and even study. The other means "to muse, meditate upon, study" (Ps. 119:15, 23, 48. 78, 148). Biblical meditation is pondering over God's Word (Jos. 1:8; Ps. 1:2; 119:12, 23, 48, 78, 148), His works in His Word (Ps. 143:5), and His ways as gleaned from His Word (Ps. 119:15). God wants His children to think about His Word. Biblical meditation is not Eastern meditation. Eastern meditation is attempting to empty the mind. Biblical meditation is filling the mind with God's Word and ways.

Outline the Passage To think seriously about the Bible, start with literary units. The two major literary units in the Bible are paragraphs and narratives. Some Bibles are printed in paragraphs instead of verses. Some editions of the NKJV designate the beginning of the paragraph by putting the first verse of the paragraph in bold type. Narratives are simply stories. After you have determined the literary unit, outline it.

Outline Psalm 1. Stop. Before you read the next sentence in this book, open the Bible and outline Psalm 1. Psalm 1 contains two parts. It begins by talking about a blessed man (Ps. 1:1-3).

Then it talks about an ungodly man (Ps. 1:4-6).

Summarize the Passage After you outline the passage, summarize it in a single sentence. You do that by asking two questions: what is the author talking about (subject) and what is he saying about that subject (an assertion)? What is the author of Psalm 1 talking about; what is his subject? Psalm 1 is talking about two kinds of people. What is he saying about those two kinds of people? He is saying the blessed man, who meditates in the Law of God, is planted like a tree and the ungodly, who do not meditate in the law, are like the chaff blowing in the wind. The blessed are stable and the ungodly are unstable.

Apply the Passage Think about how you would apply the principles of the passage.

The problem for modern Americans is that meditation is a lost art. From the moment we get up in the morning until we go to bed at night, our minds are bombarded with a million messages from myriad directions. We read the paper, listen to the radio, see billboards, talk to our friends, talk on our cell phones, watch TV, spend hours in front of a computer, etc. Our minds are saturated. What we have lost is the practice of meditating *on Scripture*.

Believe It

The Miracles The second thing to be done before you can obey the Bible is to believe it. "I have been crucified with Christ; it is no longer I who live, but Christ lives in me; and the *life* which I now live in the flesh I live by faith in the Son of God, who loved me and gave Himself for me" (Gal. 2:20). Hebrews 11 is the Hall of Fame of faith, not the whole of fame of obedience. Faith comes before obedience. The challenges to believing the Bible are miracles and material that strikes people as unfair.

Some people have a hard time believing the Bible because of the miracles in it. For example, do you believe there was a universal flood, that the children of Israel crossed the Red Sea on dry ground, or that a whale swallowed Jonah? A verse in the Bible answers every objection to the miraculous. Genesis 1:1 says, "In the beginning, God created the heavens and the earth." If you believe that one verse, none of the miracles in the Bible are a problem.

By the way, there is evidence of a universal flood. Fossils of marine creatures, such as fish and clams, are buried even on high mountains. There are universal flood stories recorded by all the major people groups on the earth.

As for the crossing of the Red Sea, "Florida State oceanographer Doron Nof set out to investigate whether the parting of the Red Sea is 'plausible from a physical point of view.' Using a common phenomenon called the wind set-down effect, he found that 'a northwesterly wind of 20 m/s blowing for 10-14 h is sufficient to cause a sea level drop of about 2.5m.' Such a drop in sea level, Nof speculates, might have exposed an underwater ridge, which the Israelites crossed as if it were dry land. Although the event is plausible, Nof estimated that the likelihood of such a storm occurring in that particular place and time of year is less than once every 2,400 years" (https://slate.com/human-interest/2009/04/scientific-explanations-for-the-parting-of-the-red-sea-the-10-plagues-and-the-burning-bush.html).

The Bible does not say a whale swallowed Jonah. It says, "The Lord had prepared a great fish to swallow Jonah" (Jonah 1:17). The Lord could've prepared a fish with wall-to-wall carpeting and air conditioning. By the way, there are stories of people being swallowed by a large fish and surviving. Genesis 18:14 asks, "Is anything too hard for the Lord?"

Injustice Some people have a hard time because they believe things happened in the Bible that were unfair, such as the destruction of the Canaanites. The one verse in the Bible that answers those kinds of objections is Genesis 18:25, which says, shall not the judge of all the earth do right?" Concerning the Canaanites, God gave them 400 years to repent (Gen. 15:13). Furthermore, they deserve to be judged because of their gross idolatry, immorality, and their sacrificing children to idols. What about the fact that innocent children were killed? Children go to heaven when they die. So God did them a favor by not letting them become adults and idolaters like their parents and be judged.

Obey It

John "Blessed is he who reads and those who hear the words of this prophecy, and keep those things which are written in it" (Rev. 1:3). This verse talks about people who hear, read, obviously understand, believe, and obey the Scripture. Those who keep the Word are those who not only hear but also do what this book says do. They do not hear and forget, nor do they hear and neglect. They hear and "keep," that is, "obey from the heart." The obedient will be blessed.

James "Be doers of Word and not hearers only, deceiving yourselves" (Jas. 1:22). Hearing the Word is probably a reference to hearing the Word read and taught in an assembly of believers (Hodges). Believers are to hear and heed the Word of God. What follows in the remainder of this paragraph are two reasons why believers should do the Word.

First, they will be deceived if they hear the Word and do not do what it says. James puts it like this: "For if anyone is a hearer of the Word and not a doer, he is like a man observing his natural face in a mirror where he observes himself, goes away and immediately forgets what kind of man he was" (Jas. 1:23-24). This passage is usually taken to mean that a man looks in a mirror and sees his "flaw" (Blue), "shortcomings and defects" (Barnes), "blemishes, imperfections, deformities, and impurities" (Clarke). If that is the case, notice James says he is like a "man;" he does not say like a "woman." The Greek word rendered "man" means "male." A female would never do what James says males do. If a woman looks into a mirror and sees anything wrong, she immediately corrects it, but men do not necessarily do that. A male of the species may look in a mirror, see a problem, not correct it, walk away, and soon even forget that he had not shaved or that his hair was not combed. Likewise, when believers hear the Word of God and do not do what it says, they risk being deceived. The Greek word translated "deceived" means "to miscalculate, to reason falsely, to mislead."

The occupational hazard of attending a Bible-teaching church is that believers could conclude they are okay just because they hear the Word. They could take pride in hearing the Word, but those who do not do what it says are as bad off or worse off than those who do not hear it. They end up deceived.

James gives a second reason why a believer should obey the Word. He says, "But he who looks into the perfect law of liberty and continues in it and is not a forgetful hearer but a doer of the work, this one is blessed in what he does" (Jas. 1:25). This verse outlines the process to obedience. It begins with looking into the perfect law of liberty. The Greek word translated "look" is not talking about a mere glance; it means "to stoop and look." The idea is to bend over something to get a closer look at it. This refers to the close observation of the text of Scripture. The perfect law of liberty is the law of love (Mayor; Mitton). The law of love liberates! It is the complete, perfect law.

The next step to obedience is to "continue" in the Word. This is not the usual Greek word for "continue" in the New Testament. This particular word means "to continue beside." Alford refers to Wiesinger's remarks that the idea is not so much about continuing to observe it in action as it is about observing it in attention. In other words, this is a reference to meditation. After observing what the Word says, a believer needs to linger *beside* it, thinking through what it means and how to apply it.

The third and final step in obedience is to do the work. The Bible was written not just for meditation and contemplation but for action. Aristotle wrote in the front of one of his books, "This book was written for action, not discussion." Believers who do what the Word of God says will be blessed. They will hear God speak. They will be blessed with endurance, completeness, maturity, insight, wisdom, happiness, and righteousness (Jas. 1:3, 4, 5, 12, 19). They will be blessed, indeed.

Share It

"Now, Saul was consenting to his death. At that time, a great persecution arose against the church which was at Jerusalem; and they were all scattered throughout the regions of Judea and Samaria, except the apostles" (Acts 8:1). After the stoning of Stephen, great persecution fell on the church at Jerusalem. As a result of the persecution, the believers in Jerusalem were scattered throughout the regions of Judea and Samaria. Luke says *all* were scattered except the apostles. "Therefore those who were scattered went everywhere preaching the word" (Acts 8:4). The conclusion ("therefore") is that those scattered preached the Word everywhere they went.

Summary: Believers are to feed on the Word of God so that they may grow by listening to it, reading it, meditating on it, believing it, and obeying it, which includes sharing it.

"Now, O Israel, listen to the statutes and the judgments which I teach you to observe, that you may live, and go in and possess the land which the LORD God of your fathers is giving you" (Deut. 4:1). "But be doers of the word, and not hearers only, deceiving yourselves" (Jas. 1:22).

On that blank page in the back of your Bible, write, "5. The Word" and after it, "James 1:22."

Part of obeying the book is sharing the book. In the book I wrote on how to study the Bible, I concluded by saying, *"I sincerely doubt that you will ever know the truth of the Word of God until you have experienced it and taught it several times."*

"One day, a young Christian came to a mission station in Korea to visit the pastor who had been instrumental in his conversion. After the customary greeting, the missionary asks the reason for his coming. 'I've been memorizing some verses in the Bible,' he said. 'And I want to quote them for you.' He had brought hundreds of miles just to recite some Scripture verses to his father in the faith. The pastor listened as he repeated the entire sermon on the Mount without error. He commended the young man for his remarkable feat of memory. Then he cautioned that the young man must 'say' the Scriptures and practice them. With a glowing face, the man responded, 'Oh, that is how I learned them. I tried to memorize them, but they wouldn't stick. So, I hit on this plan. First, I would learn a verse. Then, I would talk to a neighbor who was not a Christian and practice it on him. After doing that, I found I could remember it'" (*Our Daily Bread,* 11/18/1981).

Chapter 6

SPIRITUAL BASICS: UNDERSTANDING THE BIBLE

All who read the Bible want to understand the Bible correctly, but obviously, not everyone who reads the Bible does that. Even Bible teachers do not always understand the Bible correctly. Just listen to them. They differ from each other. It can both be right.

To complicate matters, frankly, the Bible can be difficult to understand. Peter said Paul was difficult to understand. Peter said, "Therefore, beloved, looking forward to these things, be diligent to be found by Him in peace, without spot and blameless; and consider *that* the longsuffering of our Lord *is* salvation—as also our beloved brother Paul, according to the wisdom given to him, has written to you, as also in all his epistles, speaking in them of these things, in which are some things hard to understand, which untaught and unstable *people* twist to their own destruction, as *they do* also the rest of the Scriptures" (2 Pet. 3:14-16).

Wow! If Peter had difficulty understanding Paul, what hope was there for me? What is necessary to understand the Bible? Several things are involved, but two issues are especially essential.

Salvation

Jesus The first thing essential to knowing the Scripture is knowing the Lord. Jesus told Nicodemus, "Most assuredly, I say to you unless one is born again, he cannot see the kingdom of God" (Jn. 3:3). Jesus is teaching that except people experience this second birth, they cannot "see" the kingdom of God. The Greek word translated "see" means "perceive, discern." In other words, without the new birth, there is no understanding of spiritual things. The statement implies incapability rather than prohibition. Jesus is not saying such an individual would be arbitrarily barred, but rather that he is inherently incapable, just as a blind man cannot see the sun (Tenney).

Paul Paul says, "But the natural man does not receive the things of the Spirit of God. For they are foolishness to him. Nor can he know them, because they are spiritually discerned" (1 Cor. 2:14). The natural man is the unsaved man. According to Jude, he does not possess the Holy Spirit (see Jude 19, where the word "natural" is translated "sensual"). The unsaved person does not receive the things of the Spirit of God. The Greek word translated "receive" has the connotation of welcome, being the usual word for receiving a guest (Morris).

Furthermore, unsaved people do not welcome or receive the truths the Holy Spirit reveals because they consider them foolish. The Greek word translated "foolish" means "dull, insipid, tasteless, stupid." The unsaved considers the preaching of the cross (1 Cor. 1:18) and the deep things of God (1 Cor. 2:10) to be foolishness.

Paul adds that the unsaved do not have the ability, the power, or the capacity to grasp the Word of God. The Word of God is spiritually discerned. It requires characteristics that he does not possess. The process is beyond him. As the Holy Spirit reveals the truths of God to those who wrote them, a person must have the Holy Spirit to discern and comprehend the truths of God.

The issue is not that he does not or will not; he cannot. Nor is the issue that the unsaved person cannot understand the facts of the message of God. He cannot examine them and draw correct conclusions from them. His evaluation is eschewed. The Word of God is to him silly nonsense. The natural man's attitudes and appetites are not right.

Martin Luther said, "Man is like a pillar of salt, like Lot's wife. He is like a log in a stone. He is like a lifeless statue which uses neither eyes nor mouth, neither senses nor heart unless he is enlightened, converted, and regenerated by the Holy Spirit." Or, as someone else has pointed out, "A real love letter is ridiculous to everyone but the sender and the recipient."

Shortly after color television was introduced in this country, a viewer wrote a letter to his local television station complaining that the pictures were still coming to him in black and white. Accusing the management of deliberately misleading the public, he demanded an apology. The broadcast official kindly explained to the disgruntled customer that color pictures could not be picked up on his ordinary black-and-white set. The difficulty was not in their transmission but in his receiver. Likewise, the difficulty is not with the Word of God but in the ability to receive in the natural man.

The point is unbelievers do not understand the Word of God. Understanding the Bible is a spiritual issue. Only those born of the Spirit can truly understand it.

Prayer

Knowing the Lord is essential, but it's not enough. Peter knew the Lord but still had difficulty understanding some things in the Scripture. Understanding the Scripture involves the work of God.

God's Work When the Lord asked the apostles, "Who do you say that I am? Simon Peter answered and said, 'You are the Christ, the Son of the living God'" (Mt. 16:15-16). "Jesus answered and said to him, 'Blessed are you, Simon Bar-Jonah, for flesh and blood has not revealed *this* to you, but My Father who is in heaven'" (Mt. 16:17). The expression "flesh and blood" means humanity in contrast to God. Peter had not received his knowledge from any human source.

When Peter first met Jesus, his brother Andrew told him Jesus was the Messiah (Jn. 1:41; see also 3:17; 14:33). How can Jesus say that no human revealed that to Peter? God may have used a human instrument, but God illuminated Peter. Peter's conclusion about Christ was not a secondhand opinion learned from others. God the Father revealed to Peter that Jesus was the Messiah, the Son of God (Mt. 11:25-27).

In the Upper Room, Jesus said, "However, when He, the Spirit of truth, has come, He will guide you into all truth" (Jn. 16:13). The Holy Spirit would *lead* them into truth. They could refuse to follow.

When the Holy Spirit came to do His work, and they cooperated with Him, they would discover all truth needed to be mature saints and thoroughly equipped servants (2 Tim. 3:16-17).

Prayer So, what do we have to do with the Spirit of God to guide us into all truth? The answer is depend on Him. The psalmist prayed, "Open my eyes that I may see wondrous things from Your law" (119:18). The Hebrew word translated "open" means to "uncover, reveal, disclose," and the one rendered "marvelous" means "to be beyond one's power, difficult to understand, wonderful, marvelous." The psalmist is praying for the Lord to reveal the difficult-to-understand, yet wonderful, things in His Word.

The point is to understand the Word of God. Ephesians says, "Therefore do not be unwise, but understand what the will of the Lord is."

Context

How do we know when the Holy Spirit has guided us? Just because we pray does not mean we are cooperating with His guidance. What determines correct interpretation?

The correct interpretation is the author's intended meaning. The meaning is not what I think it means or what somebody else says it means, but what the author intended the meaning to be. How is the author's intended meaning determined? The answer to that is context.

Let me illustrate. Words have different meanings. For example, the word "trunk" can mean the front end of an elephant, the back in the car, a chest in the attic, part of a tree, or even part of the human body. The dictionary gives us the various meanings of the word. In written material, how do I know which meaning the author intended? The answer is context. Suppose someone gave you something and said, put this in the trunk? Does she mean the trunk in the attic or the trunk of the trunk of the car? If she's talking about the suitcase she is taking on the trip they are about to take, she means the back end of the car and not the trunk in the attic.

The meaning of the word "saved" is determined by the context. In the Bible, the word "saved" means "delivered." It is used of people being delivered out of trouble. This poor man cried out, and the LORD heard *him* and saved him out of all his troubles (Ps. 34:6). It is used of people being delivered out of their distress. Then they cried out to the LORD in their trouble, *and* He saved them out of their distresses" (Ps. 107:13). It is used of people being delivered out of disease. "The prayer of faith shall save the sick" (Jas. 5:15). It is used of people being delivered from death. "But the midwives feared God and did not do as the king of Egypt commanded them, but saved the male children alive" (Ex. 1:17). "And unless those days were shortened, no flesh would be saved" (Mt. 24:22). "Paul said to the centurion and the soldiers, 'Unless these men stay in the ship, you cannot be saved'" (Acts 27:31).

Spiritually, the Bible speaks of having been saved. "For by grace you have been saved through faith" (Eph. 2:8; see Titus 3:5).

It speaks of "being saved." "For the message of the cross is foolishness to those who are perishing, but to us who are being saved, it is the power of God" (1 Cor. 1:18; see also Rom. 5:10). It says believers "will be saved." "And do this, knowing the time, but now it is high time to wake out of sleep; for our salvation is near than we first believed" (Rom. 13:11; 1 Pet. 1:5). Theologians explained this by saying believers have been saved from the penalty of sin; they are being saved from the power of sin; they will be saved from the presence of sin.

The meaning of the word "justification" is determined by the context. In Romans, justification is by faith. "Therefore, having been justified by faith, we have peace with God through our Lord Jesus Christ" (Rom. 5:1). In James, justification is by works. "Was not Abraham our father justified by works when he offered Isaac his son on the altar?" (Jas. 2:21). "Likewise, was not Rahab the harlot also justified by works when she received the messengers and sent them out another way?" (Jas. 2:25). Is that a contradiction? No! Paul says, "For if Abraham was justified by works, he had something to boast about, but not before God" (Rom. 4:2). Justification by faith is before God; justification by works is before people.

The meaning of the word "righteous" is determined by the context. In Romans, the "righteousness of God is through faith in Jesus Christ to all and on all who believe" (Rom. 3:22). Yet James says, "So then, my beloved brethren, let every man be swift to hear, slow to speak, slow to wrath; for the wrath of man does not produce the righteousness of God" (Jas. 1:19-20). That verse teaches that you that you have to be slow to wrath to produce the righteousness of God in your life. Which is it? In my righteous by faith or is my righteous by living a righteous life? The word "justification" means "to be declared righteous." By faith, I have been declared righteous before God. Now that I have that righteousness before God, I need to practice righteousness. Theologians call this positional righteousness and practical righteousness. I am a citizen by birth. I am a good citizen by my conduct. Bad conduct does not negate citizenship.

The meaning of the word "redemption" is determined by the context. In one passage, the Bible speaks as if redemption was in the past and, in another, as if it is in the future. "In Him, we have redemption through his blood, the forgiveness of sins, according to the riches of His grace" (Eph. 1:7; Col. 1:14; Rom. 3:24). "Now when these things begin to happen, look up and lift up your heads, because your redemption draws near" (Lk. 21:28). "And do not grieve the Holy Spirit of God, by whom you were sealed for the day of redemption" (Eph. 4:30). Is our redemption past or is it future? Paul explains, " Not only *that,* but we also who have the firstfruits of the Spirit, even we ourselves groan within ourselves, eagerly waiting for the adoption, the redemption of our body" (Rom. 8:23). When you trusted Christ, you were redeemed. In that sense, redemption is in the past; you have been forgiven of your sins. Your body will be redeemed when Christ returns.

The meaning of the word "sanctification" is determined by the context. The Greek word translated "sanctified" means "set apart." The Bible speaks as if that has already been done. "But of Him, you are in Christ Jesus, who became for us wisdom from God—and righteousness and sanctification and redemption" (1 Cor. 1:30). The same author who wrote that said sanctification was still a work in process. "Now, may the God of peace Himself sanctify you completely" (1 Thess. 5:23). In this case, the explanation is simple. I've been set apart to the Lord, but as I grow in the Lord, I am more and more set apart to Him.

If all of this sounds confusing, remember this: a human has a spirit, a soul, and a body. "Now may the God of peace Himself sanctify you completely; and may your whole spirit, soul, and body be preserved blameless at the coming of our Lord Jesus Christ" (1 Thess. 5:23). The believer's spirit has been saved, justified, made righteous, redeemed, and sanctified (set apart) to the Lord. That is the settled, secure issue. The believer's soul (the Greek word "soul" means "life")is being saved, made righteous, and sanctified (set apart). The believer's body will be saved and redeemed when Christ returns.

The meaning of the phrase "know the Lord" is determined by the context. According to the Bible, when you trust Christ, you know the Lord. "And this is eternal life, that they may know you, the only true God, and Jesus Christ whom you have sent" (Jn. 17:3). Yet, 25 years after Paul met Christ on the Damascus Road, he wrote, "that I may know Him and the power of His resurrection, and the fellowship of His sufferings, being conformed to His death" (Phil. 3:10). The event is not hard to understand. It is one thing to know a person initially, having met them. It is another thing to know someone intimately. In Philippians 3:10, Paul, who initially met the Lord on the road to Damascus, expresses a desire to know the Lord intimately.

That distinction is critical in 1 John 2, where John says, "Now by this we know we know Him, if we keep His commandments. He who says, 'I know Him,' and does not keep His commandments, is a liar and the truth is not in Him" (1 Jn. 2:3-4). Is John saying that if you don't keep the Lord's commandments, you don't know Him? Is he talking about knowing the Lord initially or intimately? The answer is in the context. Read the next verse. "But whoever keeps His word, truly the love of God is perfected in him. By this we know that we are in Him. He who says he abides in Him ought himself also to walk just as He walked" (1 Jn. 2:5-6). The issue in this passage is knowing the Lord intimately, as the words "perfected in Him" and "abides in Him" indicate.

The meaning of the word "inheritance" is determined by the context. All who have trusted Jesus are heirs of God. Paul says, "And if children—heirs of God" (Rom. 8:17a). Their inheritance includes eternal life (Titus 3:4-7). Paul adds, "and joint-heirs with Christ if indeed we suffer with Him that we may also be glorified together" (Rom. 8:17b). There are obviously two different heirships in this verse: the simple heir and the joint-heir. That is indicated by the fact that the requirement to be an heir is to be a son, but the condition of joint heirship is suffering.

Christian slaves are told to obey their masters, knowing that from the Lord, they will receive the "reward of the inheritance" (Col. 3:23-24). In that sense, the believer's inheritance is a reward in heaven, not heaven itself. What must believers do to receive an additional inheritance, a reward? The meek shall inherit the earth (Mt. 5:5). The righteous, who help the needy, will inherit the Kingdom (Mt. 25:34). Believers who are *rich* in faith are heirs of the Kingdom (Jas. 2:5, italics added). Those who bless others will inherit a blessing (1 Pet. 3:9). Those with faith and patience inherit the promises (Heb. 6:12, 14). The overcomer will inherit all things (Rev. 21:7). To summarize the concept of inheritance, while all believers have an inheritance, faithful believers have an additional inheritance.

Some believers will be disinherited. Three passages in Paul's epistles speak of people who do not inherit the Kingdom of God (1 Cor. 6:8-11; Eph. 5:3-4; Gal. 5:19-21). Does that mean people who do those sins will not *enter* the kingdom of God? No. In the first place, there is a difference between entering the Kingdom and inheriting the kingdom, as there is a difference between entering a house and inheriting a house. Furthermore, this is a different level of inheritance. All have an inheritance in the sense that they go to heaven, but there is an added inheritance for those who are faithful. In the Old Testament, all the tribes inherited the land. Some within the tribes received a double inheritance, and some were disinherited.

The meaning of the expression "eternal life" is determined by the context. Those who trust Christ have eternal life as a present possession. "He who believes in the Son has everlasting life and he who does not believe the Son shall not see life, but the wrath of God abides on him" (Jn. 3:36). Yet, Paul says, "Let him who is taught the word share in all good things with him who teaches.

Do not be deceived, God is not mocked; for whatever a man sows, that he will also reap. For he who sows to his flesh will of the flesh reap corruption, but he who sows to the Spirit will of the Spirit reap everlasting life" (Gal. 6:6-8). That passage says to pay the preacher and you reap everlasting life. Does that mean you buy everlasting life? Of course not; everlasting life is not quantity, that is, duration. It is quality. Those who serve the Lord reap a quality of eternal life that others don't. In other words, this is speaking about rewards. Read the next verse, which says, "And let us not grow weary while doing good, for in due season we shall reap if we do not lose heart" (Gal. 6:9).

There are more illustrations, but the point is that words have different meanings in different contexts. The context determines the meaning of words. The context of the book also determines the meaning of a paragraph and the context of a book in the Bible is determined by the context of the Bible.

Summary: Keys to understanding the Bible include knowing the Lord, depending on the Lord, and determining the author's intended meaning by the context of what he has written.

Assuming you know the Lord, when you read the Bible, the first thing to do is pray that the Lord will give you an understanding of His Word and then pay attention to the context.

On that blank page in the back of your Bible, under "Basics," write "6, Understanding, and after that, "Ephesians 5:17," which says, "Therefore do not be unwise, but understand what the will of the Lord is."

This does not solve all the problems of interpretation. Remember what Peter said about Paul. He said some things were hard to understand. Then he added, "Which untaught and unstable *people* twist to their own destruction, as *they do* also the rest of the Scriptures" (2 Pet. 3:16).

Some things need to be taught. In other words, sometimes, we need to be taught because the context does not give all the answers. Inheritance is an illustration. To understand that subject, you need to understand everything the Scripture says about it, beginning with the Old Testament.

So, pray for understanding, pay attention to the context, and learn from teachers, but the aim is to understand God's will.

That does not solve all the problems either. Remember, even Peter had a problem understanding Paul. There will be things you don't understand. In the final analysis, focus on the things you do understand.

D. L. Moody once said, "A man came to me with what he felt was a very difficult passage and said, 'Mr. Moody, how do you explain it?' 1 said, 'I don't explain it.' 'But how do you interpret it?' 'I don't interpret it.' 'Well, how do you understand it?' 'I don't understand it.' 'But what do you do with it?' 'I don't do anything with it.' 'You don't believe it?' 'Yes, I believe it.' There are lots of things I do not understand." Moody explained that there were things about his body and nature that he did not understand, so "Why should I expect to know everything spiritually."

"The secret *things belong* to the LORD our God, but those *things which are* revealed *belong* to us and to our children forever, that *we* may do all the words of this law" (Deut. 29:29). Mark Twain said, "It ain't those parts of the Bible that I can't understand that bother me, it is the parts that I do understand."

Chapter 7

SPIRITUAL BASICS: PRAYER

If you desire to live a biblical spiritual life, one of the most basic things you need to know about is prayer. A biblical spiritual life is possible because we establish a relationship with the Lord by trusting Jesus Christ for the gift of eternal life. Developing that relationship is like developing any relationship; it involves communication. God speaks to us through His Word and we talk to Him through prayer. What do we need to know about prayer?

The Definition of Prayer

A Common View What is prayer? It is common to speak about kinds of prayer. Psalm 150:1-2 speaks about praise. "Praise the LORD! Praise God in His sanctuary; Praise Him in His mighty firmament! Praise Him for His mighty acts; Praise Him according to His excellent greatness!" Psalm 107:8 mentions thanksgiving. "Oh, that men would give thanks to the LORD for His goodness and for His wonderful works to the children of men!" Some suggest that praise focuses on who God is while thanksgiving is thanking God for what He has done. That distinction is not made in the Scripture. We are to *praise* God for His *acts* and His *greatness*

(Ps. 150:2, 106:1). Perhaps praise includes thanksgiving.

Prayer, especially private prayer, should contain confession, at least periodically. "If we confess our sins, He is faithful and just to forgive us our sins and to cleanse us from all unrighteousness" (1 Jn. 1:9). Intercession is praying on behalf of another. The word "intercession" does not occur very often in the Bible, but the idea does. Jesus (Rom. 8:34; Heb. 7:25) and the Holy Spirit (Rom. 8:27) intercede for believers, and believers ought to intercede for one another (Jas. 5:16) as well as for unbelievers (Rom. 10:1).

The Biblical View In a sense, the essence of prayer is asking; it is making a request. In the New Testament, several of the Greek words translated "prayer" mean "to ask, to request, to wish," even "to beg." I first heard this definition of prayer as a young Christian. John R. Rice, a preacher I heard several times, wrote a book entitled *Prayer: Asking and Receiving*. Recently, I watched a message on YouTube by Dr. Stan Toussaint, who was one of my Greek professors in seminary. He pointed out there are six Greek words in the New Testament for prayer. While they have different nuances, they all mean "asking."

We often speak of different kinds of prayer. Confession is asking. Prayer is asking. Supplication is asking. Intercession is asking. There is a difference between thanksgiving and prayer. In Philippians 4:6, Paul said, "Let your requests be known with thanksgiving." Thanksgiving may be part of your talking to the Lord, but technically, the prayer itself is asking for something.

I want to know what I have to do to get an answer to prayer. Are there requirements for getting an answer?

Verses that Designate Requirements for Answers

Abide Jesus says, "If you abide in Me, and My words abide in you, you will ask what you desire, and it shall be done for you" (Jn. 15:7). According to this verse, abiding guarantees our prayers will be answered.

The Word of God must abide in you. His Word abiding in us is His Word dwelling in us richly (Col. 3:16). It is having the Word in us to the point that we are influenced by it.

You must abide in Christ. The Greek word translated "abide" in John 15:7 is the same Greek word that was translated "continue" in John 8:31. In other words, abiding in Christ assumes you have trusted Christ for the gift of eternal life (Jn. 8:30). Having trusted Christ, you *continue* to trust Him (believers walk by faith; Gal. 2:20). John 15 illustrates that with the image of the vine and the branches. The branch *depends* on the vine (see "without Me you can do nothing" in verse 5).

Abiding also requires obedience. Jesus explains abiding in verse 10: "If you keep My commandments, you will abide in My love, just as I have kept My Father's commandments and abide in His love." Abiding in Him is obeying Him (1 Jn. 3:24).

If the requirements are met and the request is made, there is a guaranteed result. In the words of Jesus, "It shall be done for you."

God's Will John says, "Now this is the confidence that we have in Him, that if we ask anything according to His will, He hears us. And if we know that He hears us, whatever we ask, we know that we have the petitions that we have asked of Him" (1 Jn. 5:14-15).

This passage contains the same pattern of prayer that appears in John 15. The requirement in this passage is asking "*according to His will.*" This is the same as His Word abiding in us. After the requirement, there is a request. In this case, the request is stated: "If we ask anything." Again, the Word and will of God inform our prayer life. If the requirement is met and the request is made, there is a guaranteed result. In the words of John, "We have the petitions that we have asked of Him." The Word of God reveals the will of God. It is the will of God to forgive us our sins (1 Jn. 1:9).

A lady known for getting answers to prayer was asked, "What is your secret to getting answers to prayer?" She replied, "I take God at His Word, and He takes me at mine."

Faith "So Jesus answered and said to them, 'Have faith in God. For assuredly, I say to you, whoever says to this mountain, "Be removed and be cast into the sea," and does not doubt in his heart but believes that those things he says will be done, he will have whatever he says. Therefore, I say to you, whatever things you ask when you pray, believe that you receive them, and you will have them'" (Mk. 11:22-24).

This passage contains the same pattern of prayer found in John 15 and 1 John 5. The requirement in this passage is "believe." Jesus makes that point over and over again in this passage. He says, "Have faith in God" (Mk. 11:22), "believe[s] that those things He says will be done" (Mk. 11:23), "whatever things you ask when you pray, believe that you receive them" (Mk. 11:24). Three times in three verses, Jesus says "believe." In fact, it might even be suggested that the subject of the passage is faith, not prayer.

After the requirement, there is a request. In this case, the request is for a mountain to be removed into the sea. That is hyperbole for something humanly impossible. If the requirement is met and the request is made, there is a guaranteed result. In the words of Jesus, "He will have whatever he says" and "you will have them."

What kinds of things can we pray for that we know is God's will and can be confident He will answer as we believe him?

Paul prayed for spiritual knowledge. He prayed, "that the God of our Lord Jesus Christ, the Father of glory, may give to you the spirit of wisdom and revelation in the knowledge of Him, the eyes of your understanding being enlightened; that you may know what is the hope of His calling, what are the riches of the glory of His inheritance in the saints, and what *is* the exceeding greatness of His power toward us who believe, according to the working of His mighty power" (Eph. 1:17-19). Paul prayed that they would have knowledge (cf. "knowledge" in verse 17 and "know" in verse 18) and "the eyes of your understanding being enlightened that you may know" (Eph. 1:18). Teachers talk about a "teachable moment." Theologians speak about illumination. We have all said, "It dawned on me. I see it." We have all had an "ah-ha" experience.

Beginning in the middle of verse 18, Paul explains the three specific things he wants them to know, namely, the "hope of His calling" (Eph. 1:18), "the riches of the glory of *His* inheritance in the saints" (Eph. 1:18; italics added), and "the exceeding greatness of His power toward us who believe" (Eph. 1:19).

Paul prayed for insight. He says, "For this reason, we also, since the day we heard it, do not cease to pray for you, and to ask that you may be filled with the knowledge of His will in all wisdom and spiritual understanding" (Col. 1:9). Paul is praying that they be filled with the knowledge of God's will. Knowledge of the will of God comes from the Word of God.

Furthermore, Paul desired that this knowledge of God's will would be "in all wisdom and spiritual understanding." The word "insight" sums up the essence of these words. In other words, Paul is praying for not just information but insight. This insight is to be spiritual, that is, it is to be the insight into the will of God, which comes from the Holy Spirit. It is possible to have information about the will of God and not have insight into how to apply that knowledge.

Here is a starter kit on spiritual insight. It is not about you; it's about others. Jesus said He did not come to be served but to serve (Mk. 10:45). It's not about externals but internals. Jesus said it's not what goes into us but what comes out that defiles us (Mt. 15:16-20). It is not about getting; it's about giving. Jesus said it is more blessed to give than receive (Acts 20:35). It's not about the temporal but the eternal things (2 Cor. 4:16-17).

Paul prayed for power. His second prayer for the Ephesians is, "That He would grant you, according to the riches of His glory, to be strengthened with might through His Spirit in the inner man" (Eph. 3:16). Paul piles one word on top of another to emphasize the power he desires believers to experience. "Strengthened with might" means "to wax strong with power." This power is to be in the inner man through the Holy Spirit.

Paul told the Corinthians, "And lest I should be exalted above measure by the abundance of the revelations, a thorn in the flesh was given to me, a messenger of Satan to buffet me, lest I be exalted above measure. Concerning this thing, I pleaded with the Lord three times that it might depart from me. And He said to me, 'My grace is sufficient for you, for My strength is made perfect in weakness.' Therefore, most gladly, I will rather boast in my infirmities that the power of Christ may rest upon me. Therefore, I take pleasure in infirmities, in reproaches, in needs, in persecutions, in distresses, for Christ's sake. For when I am weak, then I am strong" (2 Cor. 12:7-10). Notice God told Paul His grace was sufficient and explained that (cf. "for") as His strength (2 Cor. 12:9). Paul understood that when God spoke about grace, He was talking about His power (2 Cor. 12:9).

God's power is not just in miracles. Paul describes God's power in our lives when he prays for believers to be "strengthened with all might, according to His glorious power, for all patience and longsuffering with joy" (Col. 1:11). God's power enables us to be patient with people (the meaning of the Greek word translated "longsuffering") and to endure difficult situations (the meaning of the Greek word translated "patience")—*with joy.*

Paul prayed for spiritual maturity. He prayed, "Now may our Lord Jesus Christ Himself, and our God and Father, who has loved us and given us everlasting consolation and good hope by grace, comfort your hearts and establish you in every good word and work" (2 Thess. 2:16-17). Paul's prayer for comfort refers to

2 Thessalonians 2:2, where they were shaken and troubled. Paul's prayer for them to be established goes back to 2 Thessalonians 2:3, where he told them not to be deceived, and 2 Thessalonians 2:15, where he told them to hold fast to traditions. If they held fast to the truth, it would have the practical effect of producing good works instead of instability in their lives.

"Now may the God of peace Himself sanctify you completely; and may your whole spirit, soul, and body be preserved blameless at the coming of our Lord Jesus Christ" (1 Thess. 5:23). This prayer consists of two requests. The first request is for complete sanctification. The word "sanctify" means "to set apart for God." "Many are satisfied with a partial Christianity. Some parts of their life are still worldly" (Lenski). The second request is for blameless preservation. It is a restatement of the first request from another point of view. The entire preservation of which Paul speaks is defined as preservation in "spirit, soul, and body" (1 Thess. 5:23). Every part of the believer needs to be set apart to the Lord and preserved blameless. This is another way of talking about spiritual maturity. This should be our prayer, not just for backsliders and babes, but for every believer who names the name of Christ.

"Therefore we also pray always for you that our God would count you worthy of this calling, and fulfill all the good pleasure of His goodness and the work of faith with power, that the name of our Lord Jesus Christ may be glorified in you, and you in Him, according to the grace of our God and the Lord Jesus Christ" (2 Thess. 1:11-12). This prayer consists of two basic requests (see "that" in verse 11 and "that" in verse 12). The first request asks God to do three things, all of which amount to spiritual growth; namely, they would grow in their calling to the point that God would count them worthy of it, grow in goodness, and grow in works. The second request is that they would glorify the Lord. "To glorify" means "to manifest, reflect, display." So, glorifying the name of the Lord Jesus is simply manifesting all that He is. Again, this is another way of praying for spiritual maturity.

When we pray for each other, let us pray that we grow spiritually and glorify the Lord.

Paul prayed for love. He said, "Now may the Lord direct your hearts into the love of God and into the patience of Christ" (2 Thess. 3:5). This is one of the rare instances of a prayer addressed directly to Jesus. Paul prays that the Lord would direct their hearts into the love of God. In Revelation 2:4, the Lord Himself laments that the Ephesians had left their first love. In 1 John 2:15, John commands the believers in Ephesus not to love the world. Believers can leave their first love for the Lord and latch onto some love for the world. Or, to say the same thing another way, an undue attachment to things on this earth soon chills our affection for God. For us, the ever-present danger of materialism can do that. For the Thessalonians, persecution could have done that. If we are to grow in our love for the Lord, we must not allow possessions or persecution to cause us to fail.

Let us pray for believers we know to fall in love with the Lord and patiently wait for His return without flirting with another possible lover. Love is the ultimate in maturity (Eph. 4:15).

The key to answered prayer is to look at any situation and ask, "What does God say in the Scripture that He wants done in this situation?" and ask Him to do it. The purpose of prayer is not to get man's will done in heaven but to get God's will done on earth (Mt. 6:10). That explains New Testament verses like John 15:7 and 1 John 5:14: "If you abide in Me, and My words abide in you, you will ask what you desire, and it shall be done for you" (Jn. 15:7); "Now this is the confidence that we have in Him, that if we ask anything according to His will, He hears us" (1 Jn. 5:14).

So, 1) Look at the situation. 2) Look at Scripture. 3) Then ask, "What do I know from the Scripture that God wants to do in this situation?

Let me illustrate. I know of a Christian father whose daughter was dating an unsaved fellow. The father was deeply concerned that it might get serious and that she might marry an unbeliever. So, he began to pray that they would break up as a couple. The more he prayed, the more their relationship progressed. Finally, one day, as he was struggling in prayer with the Lord, it dawned on him that technically, nothing in the Scripture said that a teenage girl couldn't date an unsaved fellow, only that she should not marry him. Furthermore, he realized that the will of God in that situation was for the fellow to get saved. That would solve everything. He liked the young man; his only complaint was that he was not a believer. So, he began to pray that the young man would trust Christ. A short time later, the young man trusted Jesus Christ as his Savior. Then the couple broke up!

This pattern is both encouraging and discouraging. It is encouraging in that if we meet God's conditions, we are assured of an answer to prayer. It is discouraging because it sounds like we have to meet His conditions to get an answer.

Verses that Delete Requirements for Answers

Paul "Be anxious for nothing, but in everything by prayer and supplication, with thanksgiving, let your requests be made known to God; and the peace of God, which surpasses all understanding, will guard your hearts and minds through Christ Jesus" (Phil 4:6-7). Is there anything about this passage that strikes you as different? There is no requirement (with the possible exception of thanksgiving). This passage says, "Let your requests be made known to God." The result is you will get the peace of God.

This passage, which has no requirement, also does not guarantee receiving the request, but we have the liberty to just ask. James says we don't have because we don't ask (Jas. 4:2). Remember, there is no guarantee, as there is in the other passages.

Jesus "Ask and it will be given to you; seek, and you will find; knock, and it will be opened to you. For everyone who asks receives, and he who seeks finds, and to him who knocks it will be opened. Or what man is there among you who, if his son asks for bread, will give him a stone? Or if he asks for a fish, will he give him a serpent? If you then, being evil, know how to give good gifts to your children, how much more will your Father who is in heaven give good things to those who ask Him!" (Mt. 7:7-11).

James "Yet you do not have because you do not ask. You ask and do not receive, because you ask amiss, that you may spend *it* on your pleasures" (Jas. 4:2a.3).

Also, remember to *just ask*. In God's sovereignty, He has a will He has revealed in His Word, but God is also a Father. Listen to Jesus: "And He said to them, 'Which of you shall have a friend, and go to him at midnight and say to him, 'Friend, lend me three loaves; for a friend of mine has come to me on his journey, and I have nothing to set before him'; and he will answer from within and say, 'Do not trouble me; the door is now shut, and my children are with me in bed; I cannot rise and give to you'? I say to you, though he will not rise and give to him because he is his friend, yet because of his persistence, he will rise and give him as many as he needs. So I say to you, ask, and it will be given to you; seek, and you will find; knock, and it will be opened to you. For everyone who asks receives, and he who seeks finds, and to him who knocks it will be opened. If a son asks for bread from any father among you, will he give him a stone? Or if *he asks* for a fish, will he give him a serpent instead of a fish? Or if he asks for an egg, will he offer him a scorpion? If you then, being evil, know how to give good gifts to your children, how much more will *your* heavenly Father give the Holy Spirit to those who ask Him!" (Lk. 11:5-13).

C. I. Scofield, the author of the *Scofield Reference Bible,* lived at the turn of the last century. One day, he looked out the window and saw a new invention coming down the street. It was a horseless carriage. He told the Lord, "I don't need one of those; my horse and carriage are fine, but I'd like to have one." The Lord answered his prayer.

Let your request be made known. Your gracious Father may give it to you.

Summary: When believers ask according to God's will, He promises to answer, but He also invites us to let our request be made known.

On that blank page in the back of your Bible, under "Basics," write "7. Prayer," and after that, "Matthew 7:7," which says, "Ask, and it will be given to you; seek, and you will find; knock, and it will be opened to you."

Listen to a committee of experts on prayer. "Call upon Me in the day of trouble; I will deliver you, and you shall glorify Me" (Ps. 50:15). "Call to Me, and I will answer you, and show you great and mighty things, which you do not know" (Jer. 33:3). "And he spoke a parable unto them to this end, that men ought always to pray, and not to faint" (LK. 18:1). "Pray without ceasing" (I Thess. 5:17). **"Praying always with all prayer and supplication in the Spirit, and watching thereunto with all perseverance and supplication for all saints; And for me" (Eph. 6:18, 19).**

E. M. Bounds was a pastor in the 18th century. He is known for writing 11 books, nine of which were on prayer. Only two were published before he died. He practiced prayer, praying from 4 AM to 7 AM. He said, "Four things let us ever keep in mind: God hears prayer, God heeds prayer, God answers prayer, and God delivers by prayer."

Chapter 8

SPIRITUAL BASICS: GROWTH

Another basic biblical truth for living a spiritual life is the concept of growth. Peter says, "Therefore, laying aside all malice, all deceit, hypocrisy, envy, and all evil speaking, as newborn babes, desire the pure milk of the word, that you may grow thereby, if indeed you have tasted that the Lord *is* gracious" (1 Pet. 2:1-3). "Grow in the grace and knowledge of our Lord and Savior Jesus Christ" (2 Pet. 3:18). Believers are to grow to Christlike spiritual maturity. Two questions need to be addressed. What does spiritual maturity look like, and what must a person do to grow to spiritual maturity?

The Goal of Spiritual Growth

The Goal In Ephesians 4:11-16, Paul reveals the goal of the spiritual life. "And He Himself gave some to be apostles, some prophets, some evangelists, and some pastors and teachers" (Eph. 4:11). God has given gifted men to the church. The apostles and prophets were the foundation of the church (Eph. 2:20). The Greek word translated "evangelist" means "one who announces the gospel." In the Greek text, pastors and teachers are inseparably linked together, indicating that these are two characteristics of the same person. The Greek word translated "pastor" means "shepherd." Shepherds exercise oversight over the flock; they provide for, protect, guide, and guard it (Robinson). A teacher, of course, gives instruction. In this case, the teacher instructs others in the Word of God (2 Tim. 3:16). These two functions are united in one person. The pastor/teacher leads by feeding and he feeds by teaching the Word of God.

Paul now turns his attention to the purpose of the gifts. He first gives the immediate purpose, "for the equipping of the saints" (Eph. 4:12a). Gifted evangelists and pastor/teachers, are to equip the saints. The verb, equip, means "to mend or repair, to furnish completely, complete, equip, prepare." The meaning here is furnishing, completing, preparing, and equipping a ship for a journey. Training is the idea (Lk. 6:40).

Next, Paul discusses the intermediate purpose. He says gifted men equip saints "for the work of ministry, for the edifying of the body of Christ, till we all come to the unity of the faith and the knowledge of the Son of God, to a perfect man, to the measure of the stature of the fullness of Christ" (Eph. 4:12c-13). If you are a believer, you are in the ministry. As believers minister to one another, they edify the body of Christ until it produces unity, knowledge of the son of God, and spiritual maturity. This is not so much a reference to individual maturity, though that's included, as it is the maturity of the whole body of Christ (Pentecost). The mature man is further described as having the measure of the stature (Greek: "maturity") of the fullness of Christ, that is, complete conformity of all believers to Christ.

In Ephesians 4:14-16, Paul states the ultimate purpose of gifted men equipping saints for their ministry. He states it first negatively (4:14), then positively (4:15-16).

He says "that we should no longer be children, tossed to and fro and carried about with every wind of doctrine, by the trickery of men, in the cunning craftiness by which whey they lie in wait to deceive" (Eph. 4:14). The ultimate purpose of all ministry, stated negatively, is that believers should not be immature infants who are easily swayed and deceived. Immature believers, lured by clever deceptions of religious counterfeits, are unstable. They are tossed to and fro and carried about (Greek: to swing around ... to be carried off course) like a wave of the sea during a storm by every new wind that blows into town. They are human tumbleweeds.

The ultimate purpose of all ministry, stated positively, is "but, speaking the truth in love, may grow up in all things. into Him who is the head—Christ" (Eph. 4:15). In short, the ultimate aim is spiritual maturity. The twin conditions for growth toward maturity are truth and love. Technically, the Greek text does not say "speaking the truth in love." It says, "Truthing in love," which includes the concept of maintaining the truth in both speech and life (Westcott; Toussaint; Robinson).

There is one more verse in this paragraph and it sounds complex and even confusing. It says, "From whom the whole body, joined and knit together by what every joint supplies, according to the effective working by which every part does its share, causes growth of the body for the edifying of itself in love" (Eph. 4:16). Paul is using the figure of the human body to illustrate the body of

Christ. Every part of the body is connected to the head—Christ. As each joint fulfills its function, the body grows in love. Paul mentions love three times in this passage (4:2, 15-16). He ends with love. The ultimate in Christ-like maturity is love. To sum up, Christlike spiritual maturity includes truth and love.

Paul informs us, "For whom He foreknew, He also predestined *to be* conformed to the image of His Son, that He might be the firstborn among many brethren" (Rom. 8:29). Paul says the goal is that Christ be formed in us (Gal. 4:19). In other words, *the goal of the spiritual life is Christ-like maturity.*

The Specifics Paul concludes, "This I say, therefore, and testify in the Lord that you should no longer walk as the rest of the Gentiles walk in the futility of their mind, having their understanding darkened being alienated from the life of God, because of the ignorance that is in them, because of the hardening of their heart, who, being past feeling, have given themselves over to licentiousness to work all uncleanness with greediness. But you have not so learned Christ, if indeed you have heard Him and have been taught by Him, as the truth is in Jesus that you put off concerning your former conduct, the old man which grows corrupt according to the deceitful lusts. And be renewed in the spirit of your mind. And that you put on the new man which was created according to God, in righteousness and true holiness" (Eph. 4:17-24).

The spiritual condition of unbelievers is that they walk in the futility of their minds because they were alienated from God. Consequently, they lived in licentiousness (excess), uncleanness, and greediness. Believers learn to put off their former way of living and a new form of living according to righteousness and true holiness. Do not walk like unbelievers in unrighteousness, but walk like the new person you are in righteousness.

Beginning in Ephesians 4:25, Paul gets specific. He provides five particular exhortations. Each consists of 1) a negative commandment, 2) a positive commandment, and 3) a reason for the positive command.

1. Walk in righteousness (Eph. 4:25-32). Walk in righteousness; speak the truth. "Therefore, putting away lying, each one speak the truth with his neighbor. Each one speak the truth with his neighbor" (Eph. 4:25). A lie is contrary to fact, spoken with the intent to deceive. We are to speak the truth in love (Eph. 4:15). It is possible to speak the truth in a harsh and harmful way that hurts and does not help. It is possible to speak the truth with grace.

Believers are members of the same body, the body of Christ. "It is as unthinkable for one Christian to lie to another as it would be for a nerve in the body to deliberately send a false message to the brain, or for the eye to deceive the rest of the body when danger is approaching" (MacDonald).

Walk in righteousness; be angry. "Be angry" (Eph. 4:26a). Not all anger is sinful. Psalms 4:4 and Ephesians 4:26 command people to "be angry." The anger in verse 26 is generally called "righteous indignation." Aristotle wrote, "Anyone can become angry, but to be angry with the right person at the right degree at the right time for the right purpose and in the right way—that is not easy." Paul got angry at idolatry (Acts 17:16: "Now while Paul waited for them at Athens, his spirit was provoked within him when he saw that the city was given over to idols"). Jesus got angry at hypocrisy (Mk. 3:5; "And when He had looked around at them with anger, being grieved by the hardness of their hearts.").

There is a danger even in righteous indignation. Righteous indignation can become sinful. Paul adds, "Do not sin. Do not let the sun go down on your wrath" (Eph. 4:26b). The Greek word translated "wrath" is the Greek word for anger, plus an added prefix. The new word created by this combination means "irritation," implying a less permanent state than anger. Don't let the sun go down on your irritation is the idea. Even if the irritation or anger is justifiable, it is not to be harbored. To do so is to allow justifiable anger to become a sin.

The reason believers should never put their heads on their pillow with anger in their hearts is what Paul says next, "nor give place to the devil" (Eph. 4:27). Anger is like a fire. It may be as small as a spark, but if it becomes a flame, it causes an explosion called wrath. If the fire "rages" out of control, it can do great damage, which is called "malice" or murder (Mt. 5:21-26). When Satan sees a spark of anger that is not extinguished with the water of forgiveness, he fans it and adds fuel to the fire. Paul warns us not to give the devil that kind of opportunity. Don't assist him; resist him. You must control your anger lest it gets out of control and controls you.

Walk in righteousness; work to give. "Let him who stole steal no longer, but rather let him labor, working with *his* hands what is good, that he may have something to give him who has need" (Eph. 4:28). Stealing is using another's labor to satisfy one's desires. Working should be using one's labor to supply another's needs. Jesus said, 'It is more blessed to give than to receive'" (Acts 20:35).

Walk in righteousness; speak to edify. "Let no corrupt communication proceed out of your mouth, but what is good for necessary edification, but what is good for necessary edification. And do not grieve the Holy Spirit of God by whom you are sealed for the day of redemption" (Eph. 4:29-30). The Greek word translated "edification" means "to build up." What comes from the believer's mouth should be good, not bad; wholesome, not worthless; redemptive, not rotten. Having received grace (Eph. 2:8), we should give grace. Moreover, speaking that tears down does not build up, does not minister grace, and grieves the Holy Spirit. He is the One who enlightens us and empowers us. When He is grieved, He cannot do His world of enlightening us and empowering us.

Walk in righteousness; be kind. "Let all bitterness, wrath, anger, clamor, and evil speaking be put away from you, with all malice and be kind to one another, tenderhearted, forgiving one another, just as God in Christ also forgave you" (Eph. 4:31-32). In place of five vicious sins, Paul commands the believer to put on three godly virtues: kindness, tenderheartedness, and forgiveness.

2. Walk in love (Eph. 5:1-5). "Therefore be followers of God as dear children. And walk in love, as Christ also loved us and gave Himself for us, an offering and a sacrifice to God for a sweet-smelling aroma" (Eph. 5:1-2). Hoehner (BKC) contends that "and"

should be translated "that is" to convey the idea that this statement explains how a believer is to imitate God, namely by walking in love. The example is that Christ loved us and gave Himself for us. Thus, this is a self-sacrificing lifestyle. When believers sacrifice their time, money, effort, comfort, or convenience to serve others, it is like a sweet-smelling perfume to God.

To further clarify, Paul contrasts the kind of life believers should live with the kind of life they should not lead. He says, "But fornication and all uncleanness or covetousness, let it not even be named among you, as is fitting for the saints, neither filthiness, nor foolish talking, nor coarse jesting, which are not fitting, but rather giving of thanks, For this you know, that no fornicator, unclean person, nor covetous man, who is an idolater, has any inheritance in the kingdom of Christ and God. Let no one deceive you with empty words, for because of these things the wrath of God omes upon the sons of disobedience. Therefore do not be partakers with them" (Eph. 5:3-7). Believers are to live a life of love and self-sacrifice and not a life of lust and self-indulgence in actions, attitudes, speech, or humor because a life of love fits a child of a loving heavenly Father and a life of lust, is worthy of disinheritance and discipline.

3. Walk in the light (Eph. 5:8-14). "For you were once darkness, but now you are light in the Lord. Walk as children of light (for the fruit of the Spirit is in all goodness, righteousness and truth) finding out what is acceptable to the Lord. And have no fellowship with the unfruitful works of

darkness. but rather expose them. For it is shameful even to speak of those things which are done by them in secret, but all things that are exposed are made manifest by the light, for whatever makes manifest is light. Therefore He says, 'Awake, you who sleep. Arise from the dead, and Christ will give you light'" (Eph. 5:8-14). Believers who are light should exhibit their light and expose the darkness. Let your light shine.

4. Walk in wisdom. "See then that you walk circumspectly, not as fools but as wise. redeem the time, because the days are evil. Therefore do not be unwise. But understanding what the will of the Lord is" (Eph. 5:15-17). Everything you need to know about the will of God is in the Word of God. When people try to discern the will of God apart from the Word of God, they often end up misguided.

Other virtues could be added. I once saw one-word banners hanging in a church. The words were joy, peace, thankfulness, godliness, unity, forgiveness, love, gentleness, wisdom, hope, generosity, compassion, patience, mutual affection, self-control, and humility. Later, I learned that the pastor was preaching a series based on these words. He called them the fruit of the Spirit.

The Requirements for Spiritual Growth

Obedience to the Word of God The first requirement for spiritual growth pertains to the Scriptures. Peter says, "Desire this pure milk of the word that you may grow thereby." The previous two chapters discussed the believer's relationship to the Scripture. Samuel

Johnson, who the Oxford Dictionary of National Biography called "arguably the most distinguished man of letters in English history," observed that people need to be reminded as much as they need to be informed. So, let's review.

1. Salvation. The first thing essential to knowing the Scripture is knowing the Lord. Jesus told Nicodemus, "Most assuredly, I say to you unless one is born again, he cannot see the kingdom of God" (Jn. 3:3). The Greek word translated "see" means "perceive, discern." In other words, without spiritual birth, there is no understanding of spiritual things.

2. Prayer. The psalmist prayed, "Open my eyes that I may see wondrous things from Your law" (Ps. 119:18).

3. Listen to It. Paul told Timothy, "Till I come, give attention to reading, to exhortation, to doctrine," that is, teaching (1 Tim. 4:13). Believers are to listen to pastors reading the Word of God. The Bible emphasizes *hearing* the Word of God preached. For example, it says, "How then shall they call on Him in whom they have not believed? And how shall they believe in Him of whom they have not heard? And how shall they hear without a preacher?" (Rom. 10:14).

4. Read It. "And there, in the presence of the children of Israel, he wrote on the stones a copy of the Law of Moses which he had written" (Josh. 8:32). God wants everyone to have access to His Word. When there was no parchment or printing, God said His Word was to be chilled in stone. Jesus repeatedly said, "Have you not read?"

5. Meditate on It. The Bible emphasizes meditation. The Lord

told Joshua to meditate in the Law day and night (Josh. 1:8). The psalmist wrote that the blessed man meditates in the Law of the Lord day and night" (Ps. 1:2). David said he meditated on the Lord in the night watches (Ps. 63:6), on all His work (Ps. 77:12; 143:5), His Word (119:148), His precepts (Ps. 119:15. 119:78), and His statues (Ps. 119:48). Psalm 119:23 declares, "Your servant meditates on Your statutes."

Believe It. "I have been crucified with Christ; it is no longer I who live, but Christ lives in me; and the *life* which I now live in the flesh I live by faith in the Son of God, who loved me and gave Himself for me" (Gal. 2:20). Hebrews 11 is the Hall of Fame of faith, not the Hall of Fame of obedience. Faith comes before obedience.

Obey it. "But be doers of the Word and not hearers only, deceiving yourselves" (Jas. 1:22). Believers need obedience, but there are two kinds of obedience. The obedience the Lord desires is not legalistic obedience to rules and regulations. It is loving obedience. Jesus says, "If you love Me, keep My commandments" (Jn. 14:15). He also says, "He who has My commandments and keeps them, it is he who loves Me. And he who loves Me will be loved by My Father, and I will love him and manifest Myself to him" (Jn. 14:21) and "If anyone loves Me, he will keep My word; and My Father will love him, and We will come to him and make Our home with him" (Jn. 14:23). The motivation for the spiritual life is love for the Lord. The obedience that results in genuine godliness is loving obedience. This is not legal obedience to a set of laws or rules. It is loving obedience to a person.

Dependence on the Spirit of God "If you abide in Me, and My words abide in you, you will ask what you desire, and it shall be done for you" (Jn. 15:7). "I am the vine, you *are* the branches. He who abides in Me, and I in him, bears much fruit; for without Me you can do nothing" (Jn. 15:5). Nevertheless, I tell you the truth. It is to your advantage that I go away; for if I do not go away, the Helper will not come to you; but if I depart, I will send Him to you" (Jn. 16:7).

"I say then: Walk in the Spirit, and you shall not fulfill the lust of the flesh" (Gal. 5:16). Paul says, "Do not walk according to the flesh but according to the Spirit. For those who live according to the flesh set their minds on the things of the flesh, but those *who live* according to the Spirit, the things of the Spirit" (Rom. 8:4b-5).

Some see spiritual life as akin to rowing a boat; it all depends on them. Others say it is like a raft; God does all the work while we are passive. The spiritual life is more like operating a sailboat. We do our part of trimming the sails and the wind (the Holy Spirit) does the actual work.

It is like growing a garden. We must hoe as if it all depends on us because it does. We must pray as if it all depends on God because it does.

Fellowship with the People of God "They continued steadfastly in the apostles' doctrine and fellowship, in the breaking of bread, and in prayers" (Acts 2:42). Paul says, "For I want you to know what a great conflict I have for you and those in Laodicea, and *for* as many as have not seen my face in the flesh that their hearts may be encouraged, being knit together in love, and *attaining* to all riches of the full assurance of understanding, to the knowledge of the mystery of God, both of the Father and of Christ in whom are hidden all the treasures of wisdom and knowledge" (Col. 2:1-3). Being knit together in love brings full understanding. The expression "knit together" suggests that God's revelation cannot be understood "in isolation from the fellowship of other Christians" (Vaughan). The revelation of God cannot be known apart from the "brotherly love within the community" (Bruce). Being part of the fellowship of believers provides examples, education, and encouragement.

Summary: Christ-like spiritual maturity, which is righteousness, love, and wisdom, is obtained by obedience to the Word of God, dependence upon the Spirit of God, and fellowship with the people of God. According to the Scripture, all three of these elements must be present to grow spiritually. It is like a three-legged stool. If one leg is missing, the stool does not work correctly.

On that blank page in the back of your Bible, under "Basics," write "8. Growth," and after that, "2 Peter 3:18," which says, "Grow in the grace and knowledge of our Lord and Savior Jesus Christ."

In the book I wrote entitled *The Spiritual Life*, I concluded that the nature of the spiritual life is a process of growing to Christ-like maturity in the context of a spiritual community. It is growing from acting in an unrighteous and unloving way to being righteous and loving.

Most Christians do not grow to spiritual maturity. In the parable of the Sower, Jesus spoke of four types of soil. Concerning one group, he said, "Now the ones *that* fell among thorns are those who, when they have heard, go out and are choked with cares, riches, and pleasures of life, and bring no fruit to maturity" (Lk. 8:14). Only one out of four endured to bear fruit (Lk. 8:15).

Tim Hansel writes: "A close friend of mine was asked back to his forty-year high school reunion. For months, he saved to take his wife back to the place and the people he'd left four decades before. The closer the time came for the reunion, the more excited he became, thinking of all the wonderful stories he would hear about the changes and the accomplishments these old friends would tell him.

"One night before he left, he even pulled out his old yearbooks and read the silly statements and the good wishes for the future that students write to each other. He wondered what ol' Number 86 of his football team had done. He wondered if any others had encountered this Christ who had changed him so profoundly. He even tried to guess what some of his friends would look like and what kind of jobs and families some of these special friends had.

"The day came to leave, and I drove them to the airport. Their energy was almost contagious. 'I'll pick you up on Sunday evening, and you can tell me all about it,' I said. 'Have a great time.'

"Sunday evening arrived. As I watched them get off the plane, my friend seemed almost despondent. I almost didn't want to ask, but finally, I said, 'Well, how was the reunion?' 'Tim,' the man said, 'it was one of the saddest experiences of my life.' 'Good grief,'

I said, more than a little surprised. 'What happened?' 'It wasn't what happened, but what didn't happen. It has been forty years, forty years—and they haven't changed. They had simply gained weight, changed clothes, gotten jobs ... but they hadn't really changed. And what I experienced was maybe one of the most tragic things I could ever imagine about life. For reasons I can't fully understand, it seems as though some people choose not to change.'

"There was a long silence as we walked back to the car. On the drive home, he turned to me and said, 'I never, never want that to be said of me, Tim. Life is too precious, too sacred, too important. If you ever see me go stagnant like that, I hope you give me a quick, swift kick where I need it—for Christ's sake. I hope you'll love me enough to challenge me to keep growing'" (Tim Hansel, *Holy Sweat*. Word Books Publisher, 1987, pp. 54-55).

Chapter 9

SPIRITUAL BASICS: THE WILL OF GOD

In the previous chapter, I concluded the discussion on spiritual maturity by saying that God is wise, so spiritually mature people are wise. According to Paul, part of being wise is understanding the will of God. "Therefore do not be unwise, but understanding what the will of the Lord is" (Eph. 5:17). What does God want us to do? How do we discover the will of God?

Confusion

Several answers to that question misuse passages of Scripture and, as a result, cause confusion concerning the will of God and how to find it.

Fleece The notion of "putting out a fleece" comes from the story of Gideon in the book of Judges. "So Gideon said to God, 'If You will save Israel by my hand as You have said—look, I shall put a fleece of wool on the threshing floor; if there is dew on the fleece only, and *it is* dry on all the ground, then I shall know that You will save Israel by my hand, as You have said.' And it was so. When he rose early the next morning and squeezed the fleece together, he wrung the dew out of the fleece, a bowlful of water. Then Gideon said to God, 'Do not be angry with me, but let me speak just once more: Let me test, I pray, just once more with the fleece; let it now be dry only on the fleece, but on all the ground let there be dew.' And God did so that night. It was dry on the fleece only, but there was dew on all the ground" (Judges 6:36-40).

The problem with Gideon's fleece was Gideon's faith. God revealed His will to Gideon earlier in the chapter: "And the Angel of the LORD appeared to him [Gideon], and said to him, 'The LORD *is* with you, you mighty man of valor!' Gideon said to Him, 'O my lord if the LORD is with us, why then has all this happened to us? And where *are* all His miracles which our fathers told us about, saying, 'Did not the LORD bring us up from Egypt?' But now the LORD has forsaken us and delivered us into the hands of the Midianites.' Then the LORD turned to him and said, 'Go in this might of yours, and you shall save Israel from the hand of the Midianites. Have I not sent you?'" (Judges 6:12-14).

Furthermore, the Lord told Gideon again he would defeat the Midianites: "So he said to Him, 'O my Lord, how can I save Israel? Indeed, my clan *is* the weakest in Manasseh, and I *am* the least in my father's house. And the LORD said to him, 'Surely I will be with you, and you shall defeat the Midianites as one man'" (Judges 6:15-16).

After all that, Gideon still said, "If now I have found favor in Your sight, then show me a sign that it is You who talk with me" (Judges 6:17). For Gideon, God's Word was not enough. He still requested a sign. In other words, He did not believe God! He plainly said, "If You will save Israel by my hand as You have said" (Judges 6:36).

Should we use a "fleece" today? No! Gideon should not have used it! God revealed His will and His promise to Gideon. Note: the fleece was not a method of determining God's will. God revealed His will to Gideon. Putting out the fleece after God had clearly revealed His will was an act of unbelief.

People use the "fleece" incorrectly today. A fellow told me that as he was lying in bed, he said to the Lord, "If it is Your will, let the light go out," and the light went out. I told him, "For that to have been a biblical fleece, you would have had to have said, 'Now let the light come back on.'"

Lots Several passages in the Old Testament and one in the New Testament speak about casting lots. In Proverbs 16:33, Solomon says, "The lot is cast into the lap, but its every decision *is* from the LORD." Casting lots consisted of writing options on stones, placing the stones in a vessel (or, as here, the lap, that is, in the fold of a garment), and shaking the container until one fell out. Proverbs 16:33 says that the one that falls out is not the result of mere chance; it is the result of the hand of the Lord.

In the Old Testament, the Lord used the casting of lots for people to determine His will (1 Sam. 14:37-42). It was used for the selection of a scapegoat (Lev. 16:8), the distribution of the duties of the priest (1 Chron. 24:5-19), and the division of the land (Josh. 18:8). It was also used to determine the duties in the Temple.

In Acts 1, casting lots determined who should replace Judas Iscariot. Thus, Matthias was not appointed by the apostles or the church but directly by the Lord. Notice what the apostles did. They looked at the Scripture (Acts 1:15-17, 21), prayed (Acts 1:24-25), and agreed as a group (Acts 1:23). The Lord had opened their minds to understand the Scripture (Lk. 24:45), and the Lord had breathed on them imparting to them the Holy Spirit until Pentecost (Jn. 20:22), at which time they were baptized by the Holy Spirit (Acts 1:5). In other words, Peter was not referring to the Psalms on his own; he was being guided into all truth by the Spirit of God.

The question is, "Should we use casting lots today to determine God's will?" No. The last incident of casting lots in the Bible is in Acts 1. After the coming of the Holy Spirit in Acts 2, there is no other case of believers casting lots. So, to determine the will of God, do not cast lots.

Circumstances Does an "open door" indicate God's will? What does the Bible say about open doors? The New Testament uses the expression "open door" five times (Acts 14:27; 1 Cor. 16:9; 2 Cor. 2:12; Col. 4:3; Rev. 3:8). In four of the five, it refers to some opportunity for gospel ministry. That is probably the meaning in the fifth occurrence.

Acts 14:27 says God "opened the door of faith to the Gentiles." In other words, God allowed the Gentiles to hear and believe the gospel.

In 1 Corinthians 16:9, Paul says, "A great and effective door has opened" to him at Ephesus. The word "door" is a figure for entrance or opportunity. In Ephesus, the opportunities were "great," that is, numerous and they were "effective," meaning productive.

In 2 Corinthians 2:12-13, Paul says, "Furthermore, when I came to Troas to preach Christ's gospel, and a door was opened to me by the Lord. I had no rest in my spirit because I did not find Titus, my brother; but taking my leave of them, I departed for Macedonia" (2 Cor. 2:12-13). When Paul got to Troas, the Lord opened a door of opportunity to preach the gospel, but he was deeply concerned about the response of the Corinthians to the letter he had written to them. So he left Troas to find out about the Corinthians. In this case, Paul walked away from an open door!

In Colossians 4:3, Paul asked the Colossians to pray for him "that God would open to us a door for the word, to speak the mystery of Christ, for which I am also in chains." The phrase "open to us a door" means "to give us an opportunity." Paul desired an opportunity to speak the Word.

In Revelation 3:7, Jesus identifies Himself as "He who opens and no one shuts and shuts and no one opens." In the next verse, He tells the Philadelphia church, "I have set before you an open door, and no one can shut it." The open door has been interpreted as the door into the eternal kingdom and as an opportunity for service. Since the figure of an open door is used elsewhere in the New Testament as an opportunity to preach the gospel, that is probably the meaning here.

The problem is an open door is not necessarily a sign that the opportunity is the will of God. Remember, Paul walked away from an open door.

Circumstances must be interpreted. In his book, *Decision-making and the Will of God*, Friesen says, "Just listen to this imaginary believable discussion concerning the 'message' God was trying to convey when lightning struck a church steeple. 'God is telling us to relocate to the suburbs.' 'Oh no, I think it's quite obvious he's saying 'no' to our expansion plans.' 'Maybe the Lord is telling us that there is a sin holding back the work in our church'" (Friesen, p. 213). Later in his book, Friesen adds, "An event cannot communicate a message apart from divine revelation" (Friesen, p. 215).

God is the supreme sovereign of the universe. Nothing happens without His knowledge and permission (Job 1-2). Yet the Scripture also allows for chance. Putting God's control and chance together is one of life's puzzles. There is no doubt that God is ultimately in control of everything, yet from a human point of view, it often seems like chance.

When Ruth gleaned in the field after the reapers, "She *happened* to come to the part of the field belonging to Boaz" (Ruth 2:3, italics added). Ruth landed on Boaz's field by "chance" (Arthur E. Cundall and Leon Morris, *Judges and Ruth*). It was a "stroke of luck" (Robert L. Hubbard, *The Book of Ruth*). God is ultimately in control of everything (Ruth 1:20-21). Yet things happen by chance (Ruth 2:3). Most scholars conclude, "Our author thinks of God as being in all of this" (Morris) or "unseen divine providence lay behind her good luck" (Hubbard).

In the parable of the Good Samaritan, Jesus said, "*by chance*, a certain priest came down that road" (Lk. 10:31, italics added).

Concerning the runaway slave Onesimus, Paul told his owner Philemon, "*Perhaps* he departed for a while for this purpose that you might receive him forever, no longer as a slave, but more than a slave, as a beloved brother" especially to me, but how much more to you, both in the flesh and in the Lord" (Phlm. 15-16, italics added). Paul said *perhaps* Onesimus ran away so Philemon would receive him as a brother.

Listening to Impressions Many say one of the major ways the Lord leads us is by an inner impression. Romans 8:14 and Galatians 5:18 speak about being led by the Spirit. Being "led by the Spirit" is often said to refer to an inner impression, an inner impulse, an inner "still, small voice," etc. The idea is that through inner impressions, the Holy Spirit leads believers into the ideal will of God.

The problem with that view is that the context of these verses does not deal with daily decisions concerning non-moral issues. Moreover, nothing in these verses or their contexts indicates that the *means* of the leading of the Holy Spirit is by an inward impression.

What does being led by the Spirit mean? In Romans 8, Paul says, "But if by the Spirit you put to death the deeds of the body, you will live. For as many as are led by the Spirit of God, these are the sons of God" (8:13-14). Notice that Romans 8:14 begins with "for," meaning it explains the previous verse. Romans 8:13 says by depending on the Holy Spirit, believers can put to death the sins committed through the body. The result is spiritual living. Furthermore, the Spirit-led life is a life of sonship (Rom. 8:14). Being "led by the Spirit" is virtually synonymous with walking according to the Spirit (Rom. 8:1, 5, 13). "Walking" highlights believers' active participation and effort in the process. "Being led" underscores the passive, submissive side of dependence. It does not eliminate the active involvement of believers. One person being led through a crowd still must put forth effort to walk. This kind of spiritual life is a life of being God's son.

In Galatians 5, Paul says, "I say then: walk in the Spirit and you shall not fulfill the lust of the flesh. For the flesh lusts against the Spirit and the Spirit against the flesh and these are contrary to one another, so that you do not do the things you wish. But if you are led by the Spirit you are not under the law" (Gal. 5:16-18). As in Romans 8, being led by the Spirit is practically synonymous with walking in the Spirit. Being led doesn't mean being carried. A blind man being led by another still has to walk. In these verses, Paul talks about the moral will of God.

Impressions are real. We all have them, but nothing in the Bible says they indicate God's will. The simple reality is that impressions can come from all kinds of places. "Do not hastily ascribe things to God. Do not easily suppose dreams, voices, impressions, visions, or revelations are from God. They may be from Him. They may be from nature. They may be from the Devil" (John Wesley, cited by J. K. Johnston, *Why Christians Sin*, Discovery House, 1992, p. 102).

Peace Another standard answer is that God lets us know His will by giving us peace. The verse used to support that notion is Colossians 3:15, which says, "And let the peace of God rule in your hearts, to which also you were called in one body; and be thankful." This verse is used to say that when you are faced with a decision, let the peace of God be the determining factor in knowing the will of God. But is that what this verse is saying?

The problem with that notion is that this verse does not say God gives us peace to indicate we have made the right decision. The Greek word translated "rule" means "to act as umpire," hence, "to arbitrate or decide." The peace of God is to be the umpire. There are personal and social aspects to letting the peace of God umpire.

Personally, the peace of God is to umpire *in our hearts*. Personal peace is the absence of anxiety (Phil. 4:6-7). If believers let this peace with God be the umpire, they will not let anything disturb them. "Let the peace of Christ act as umpire when anger, envy, and such passions arise; and restrain them. Let not those passions give the award, so that you should be swayed by them, but let Christ's peace be the decider of everything" (JFB).

Socially, the peace of God is to umpire in our relationships with other believers. Notice that Paul adds, "To which also you were called in one body." Believers are to let the peace of God rule in their hearts because they are called to peace as members of one body (Eph. 4:3). The NIV says, "Let the peace of Christ rule in your hearts since as members of one body you were called to peace. And be thankful."

Should we depend on inner peace? Paul Little tells of a young woman who had signed a teaching contract. In August, she received another offer from a school closer to where she wanted to live. So, she broke the original agreement. Had she acted on the biblical principle in Psalms 15:4, where God says that He is pleased with a person who swears to his own hurt and does not change, she would not have done that. The department chairman said her justification was, "I have a peace about it," and he commented rather sardonically, "Isn't that lovely? She's got the peace and I've got the pieces." Little says, "I believe that girl missed the will of God. She violated a principle which, if she had been alert and had applied it to her situation, would have given her clear guidance in this specific detail of her life" (Paul E. Little in a sermon, "Affirming the Will of God" in Great Sermons of the 20th Century, *Christianity Today*, vol. 33, no. 16).

This verse does not teach that peace determines the will of God. Believers have used "peace" to justify what they want to do. Jessica Hahn, the former church secretary who committed immoral acts with Jim Bakker (former host of the PTL Club), which later brought down the PTL empire, said that God gave her "real peace" about granting an interview to *Playboy Magazine* and posing for topless pictures (9/28/1987).

To sum up, God's will is not determined by using a fleece, casting lots, looking at circumstances, depending on impressions, or inner peace.

The Perfect Will of God

Romans 12:1-2 speaks of the perfect will of God. What is the perfect will of God?

Salvation It is the will of God that people be saved. Jesus said, "This is the will of the Father who sent Me, that of all He has given Me I should lose nothing but should raise it up at the last day. And this is the will of Him who sent Me, that everyone who sees the

Son and believes in Him may have everlasting life; and I will raise him up at the last day" (Jn. 6:39-40).

In 1 Timothy, Paul said, "For this *is* good and acceptable in the sight of God our Savior, who desires all men to be saved and to come to the knowledge of the truth" (1 Tim. 2:3-4).

In 2 Peter, Peter put it like this: "The Lord is not slack concerning *His* promise, as some count slackness, but is longsuffering toward us, not willing that any should perish but that all should come to repentance" (2 Pet. 3:9).

Salvation comes by believing in Jesus Christ, who died for our sins and rose from the dead (Jn. 3:16). Believing is more than believing fact; it is trusting Jesus Christ to save you. It is one thing to believe that your doctor can perform a successful operation; it is another to trust him to perform it on you.

Sanctification It is the will of God that believers be sanctified. Paul says, "For this is the will of God, your sanctification" (1 Thess. 4:3). To be sanctified means to be set apart to the Lord. Paul gives some of the specifics of sanctification.

God's will is moral purity. Paul says, "For this is the will of God, your sanctification: that you should abstain from sexual immorality" (1 Thess. 4:3). Sexual immorality is sex outside of marriage. Believers should not live according to the flesh. Peter says a believer should no longer "live the rest of *his* time in the flesh for the lusts of men, but for the will of God" (1 Pet. 4:2). John says, "And the world is passing away, and the lust of it; but he who does the will of God abides forever" (1 Jn. 2:17).

Paul also says, "Rejoice always, pray without ceasing, in everything give thanks; for this is the will of God in Christ Jesus for you" (1 Thess. 5:16-18). The last phrase, "This is the will of God in Christ Jesus for you," could go with the last command or refer to all three commands. Most expositors say that it goes with all three. Thus, God's will is for believers to rejoice always, pray without ceasing, and give thanks in every situation.

God's will is that we rejoice always. It is easy to rejoice when things are going your way. But believers are to rejoice even in trials (Jas. 1:2). Anyone can celebrate a victory; it takes a saint to rejoice during an apparent defeat. Some of the saints in Thessalonica were sorrowing for departed loved ones (1 Thess. 4:13). Others had financial problems (1 Thess. 4:11-12). All were being persecuted (1 Thess. 3:3). Yet Paul instructs them to rejoice, even during their trials. Christians can sing in the rain.

Pray without Ceasing God's will is for us to "pray without ceasing." Does that mean believers should constantly pray without interruption like a running faucet? That's impossible! "Without ceasing" does not mean without interruption. Instead, the idea is "constantly reoccurring," like a dripping faucet. This Greek term was used for a hacking cough. A person with such a cough does not cough nonstop all day long but coughs every few minutes.

Stonewall Jackson said, "I have so fixed the habit of my mind that I never raise a glass of water to my lips without asking God's blessing, never seal a letter of putting a word of prayer under the seal, never take a letter from the post without a brief sending of my thoughts heavenward, never change my classes in the lecture room without a minute's repetition for the cadets who go out and for those who come in."

God's will is "in everything, give thanks." Technically, this verse does not say "*for* everything give thanks," but "*in* everything" (Paul also says we should give thanks always "for all things" in Eph. 5:20). The concept 1 Thessalonians 5 is that believers are to give thanks in every circumstance of life, in sickness and in health; in poverty and in wealth. G. K. Chesterton said that the most important thing he learned was to take things with gratitude and not for granted.

Submission Peter says, "Therefore submit yourselves to every ordinance of man for the Lord's sake, whether to the king as supreme, or to governors, as to those who are sent by him for the punishment of evildoers and *for the* praise of those who do good. For this is the will of God, that by doing good you may put to silence the ignorance of foolish men—as free, yet not using liberty as a cloak for vice, but as bondservants of God" (1 Pet. 2:13-16).

Believers are to submit to one another in fear of God (Eph. 5:21). Wives are to submit to their husbands, as to the Lord (Eph. 5:22). Believers are to submit to church elders (Heb. 13:17). The writer to the Hebrews says, "Obey those who rule over you and be submissive, for they watch out for your souls, as those who must give account. Let them do so with joy and not with grief, for that would be unprofitable for you" (Heb. 13:17).

Concerning the churches of Macedonia, Paul says, "They first gave themselves to the Lord, and *then* to us by the will of God" (2 Cor. 8:5). The Macedonians first submitted themselves to the Lord to be obedient to Him. They were willing to do whatever the Lord desired with their lives and possessions. Then, they gave themselves to Paul and his companions to serve them in any way they could, in the will of God. God's will is for believers to obey Him and serve others. That is precisely what the Macedonians did.

Spiritual Transformation Paul writes, "I beseech you therefore, brethren, by the mercies of God that you present your bodies a living sacrifice, holy, acceptable to God" (Rom. 12:1a). Based on God's mercy, Paul entreats believers to present their bodies as sacrifices. The Greek word translated "present" is the same one in Romans 6:13, 16, 19. In Romans 6, the point is that you can use your body for either sin or righteousness. Thus, Romans 12:1 calls for obedience to God through the body. In short, use your body to obey God.

Using your body to obey the Lord is a sacrifice to Him. Romans 12:1 says, "Present your bodies a *living* sacrifice." The Greek text says, "Present your bodies a sacrifice," and adds three phrases to describe such an action. It is living, holy, and acceptable to God. The Old Testament animal sacrifice was dead. By contrast, the presentation of our bodies is a living sacrifice. "Living" here is more than just physical life, however. Believers have been raised with Christ to walk in "newness of life" (Rom. 6:4). Our sacrifice is spiritually living.

Using your body to obey the Lord is holy; it is set apart to the Lord. Consequently, our sacrifice is acceptable to God. God is well pleased with the presentation of our bodies. He delights in such sacrifices.

Paul adds, "which is your reasonable service" (Rom. 12:1b). Our sacrifice is further described as our "reasonable service." The Greek word translated "reasonable" is the word from which we get the English word "logic." In light of God's great mercies, a life of obedience is rational and reasonable.

Romans 12:1 is often used to urge believers to "dedicate" themselves to the Lord as an act of consecration. Though that may benefit some, it is not what the verse describes. This verse calls for a *life* of obedience. You can *decide* to do that in a church service, but it can only be done *as you obey*.

Paul continues, "And do not be conformed to this world" (Rom. 12:2a). Paul exhorts believers not to be continually molded and fashioned by this present, passing age. In an auto plant, a huge piece of flat metal is fed into a massive press that comes down upon it with unbelievable pressure. The sheet of metal is conformed to the mold of the press. Out comes the hood of a Chevy or a Ford.

Paul says, "Therefore do not be unwise, but understanding what the will of the Lord is" (Eph. 5:17). The word "therefore" indicates a conclusion from what precedes. Because the days are evil, believers must not be unwise; instead, they should understand the will of God. The spirit of this age is selfishness. People are obsessed with their happiness or their desires being met. That is conformity to this world.

Rather than being conformed to this age, Paul writes, "But be transformed by the renewing of your mind" (Rom. 12:2b). Instead of being molded into the shape of this age, the believer should be transformed from the inside out by the renewing of the mind.

This is no doubt a reference to the "spiritual mindedness" mentioned earlier (Rom. 8:4). As the mind, the heart, and will of believers are fixed and focused on the Word of God in general and Christ in the Word in particular, they are transformed more and more into Christ-likeness (2 Cor. 3:18, the only other place in Paul's writing where the word "transformed" appears).

This transformation results in "that you may prove what is that good and acceptable and perfect will of God" (Rom. 12:2c). By being changed through a renewed mind and obedience, you will prove in your experience the will of God. This will is further described as good, acceptable, and perfect. The Greek word translated "perfect" means "to reach its end, finished, complete." Being transformed and obedient results in God's complete will, which is good and pleasing to Him.

Believers need to think like God thinks so they will act as God wants them to act.

The paraphrase of J. B. Phillips captures the message of these two verses: "With eyes wide open to the mercies of God, I beg you, my brothers, as an act of intelligent worship to give Him your bodies as a living sacrifice consecrated to Him and acceptable by Him. Don't let the world around you squeeze you into its mold, but let God remold your minds from within so that you may prove and practice that the plan of God for you is good, meets all His demands, and moves toward the goal of true maturity."

For example, Paul says slaves are to serve "not with eyeservice, as men-pleasers, but as bondservants of Christ, doing the will of God from the heart" (Eph. 6:6).

To sum up, the perfect will of God is our salvation, sanctification, submission, and spiritual transformation. The perfect will of God is our transformation into the image of Christ; it is spiritual maturity. What you need to know about the perfect will of God is in the Word of God. God's Word has revealed 100% of God's will. As John Calvin said, "His will is not to be sought anywhere else than in His Word."

The Personal Will of God

Immediately after speaking about the will of God for all believers, Paul starts talking about people in more personal terms, not in general terms. He describes a more personal will of God.

Service "For I say, through the grace given to me, to everyone who is among you, not to think of himself more highly than he ought to think, but to think soberly as God has dealt to each one a measure of faith" (Rom. 12:3). Having said the perfect will of God is the renewal of our minds (Rom. 12:2), Paul speaks about of the way we think about ourselves. Believers are to think of themselves realistically. The phrase "a measure of faith" is usually taken to be the equivalent of "gift." Thus, Paul is saying that believers are to think of themselves according to the gift they have received.

When believers first trust Christ, they are given a spiritual gift. That gift should determine their estimate of themselves and their service in the body of Christ. Thus, they will have a sane, sober estimate of themselves and won't think too highly of themselves; that is, they won't be puffed up with self-importance. Paul thought of himself in terms of his spiritual gift. Paul was an apostle by the will of God (1 Cor. 1:1; 2 Cor. 1:1; Eph. 1:1; Col. 1:1; 2 Tim. 1:1).

So, serve the Lord "Having then gifts differing according to the grace that is given to us, let us use them" (Rom. 12:6). The ultimate aim is not just sober thinking about yourself and your gift, but your service with that gift in the body of Christ. God has sovereignly given you a gift, and His will is for you to use it. Paul then mentions seven gifts.

How do you identify your spiritual gift? For every gift, there is a corresponding responsibility. For example, there is a gift of giving, but all believers are to give. There is a gift of exhortation, but all are to exhort one another daily. There is a gift of mercy, but all are to show mercy. As you fulfill your responsibility in service, you will discover that you particularly enjoy one type of service and that you are good at it. Others will also recognize your giftedness.

Suffering It is the will of God for some believers to suffer. Peter says, "For *it is* better, if it is the will of God, to suffer for doing good than for doing evil" (1 Pet. 3:17). Notice that Peter says, "*If* it is the will of God," indicating that it may *not* be. Suffering for righteousness is not God's usual will, but if the unlikely happens (the Greek construction in verse 17 is a fourth-class condition, which means it is unlikely to happen), it is not a matter of blind chance. If suffering comes, it is the will of God.

The Gospel of John records that Jesus said to Peter, "Most assuredly, I say to you, when you were younger, you girded yourself and walked where you wished; but when you are old, you will stretch out your hands, and another will gird you and carry you where you do not wish." John explains, "This He spoke, signifying by what death he would glorify God" (Jn. 21:18-19a). The Lord tells Peter that when he was young, he fastened his belt and went where he wished, but in old age, he would not do either; he would be restrained and no longer master of his movements. In other words, the Lord is telling Peter that when he was younger, he moved about unrestricted, but in his old age, he will stretch forth his hands, that is, he will be helpless and seeking help. Another shall gird him, that is, he shall be bound as a "condemned criminal" and carried where he does not want to go, namely to a violent death.

"And when He had spoken this, He said to him, 'Follow Me'" (Jn. 21:19b). The fact that the next verse says that Peter turned around indicates this is to be taken literally, although the figurative meaning should not be totally excluded. At any rate, Peter began to follow the Lord.

"Then Peter, turning around, saw the disciple whom Jesus loved following, who also had leaned on His breast at the supper, and said, 'Lord, who is the one who betrays You?' Peter, seeing him, said to Jesus, 'But Lord, what about this man?'" (Jn. 21:20-21). Peter looked at John, who is identified as the one who leaned on Jesus' bosom and asked who would betray Him. Peter wanted to know if John would also suffer a violent death.

"Jesus said to him, 'If I will that he remain till I come, what is that to you? You follow Me'" (Jn. 21:22). Jesus told him in no uncertain terms that if it were His will for one to suffer and another to wait, that was none of Peter's business. Some suffer; some do not.

In his first epistle, Peter says, "Therefore let those who suffer according to the will of God commit their souls *to Him* in doing good, as to a faithful Creator" (1 Pet. 4:19). If you are suffering according to God's will, that is, not because you did something wrong (1 Pet. 4:15), but because you did something right (you were suffering for righteousness sake, for Christ's sake—1 Pet. 4:14), then trust yourself to God by doing good in every area of your life.

Martin Luther said, "Go on in faith and love; if the cross comes, take it; if it comes not, do not seek it."

A Specific Place Does God have a specific place for you to be? As a general rule, you should maintain your life situation. Paul says, "But as God has distributed to each one, as the Lord has called each one, so let him walk. And so I ordain in all the churches. Was anyone called while circumcised? Let him not become uncircumcised. Was anyone called while uncircumcised? Let him not be circumcised. Circumcision is nothing, and uncircumcision is nothing, but keeping the commandments of God is what matters" (1 Cor. 7:17-19). Believers should remain in the external circumstances they were in when they were saved. One's Jewishness or Gentileness should also be maintained. Bodily marks that indicate a commitment before conversion are insignificant. They do not have to be removed.

Paul goes on to say, "Let each one remain in the same calling in which he was called. Were you called while a slave? Do not be concerned about it, but if you can be made free, rather use it. For he who is called in the Lord while a slave is the Lord's freed man.

Likewise, he who is called while free is Christ's slave. You were bought at a price; do not become slaves of men. Brethren, let each one remain with God in that calling in which he was called" (1 Cor. 7:20-24). One's slave/free status should be maintained.

To paraphrase, stay in the occupation you were in when you were saved. A slave can be a good Christian. A freedman can also be a good Christian. In fact, a slave is the Lord's freedman. He is freed from sin, and a freedman is the Lord's slave. Both slaves and freedmen are bought with a price—the blood of Christ. So, don't become a slave to men by letting social relationships interfere with the relationship you have with the One who bought you. Paul closes this section with the same principle formulated in verse 17, only this time he adds "with God" (see also 1 Cor. 7:20). Let believers walk before God in the external circumstances they were in when they got saved, unless, of course, the situation is sinful.

As a general rule, your life's situation should remain the same. Jews should remain circumcised, and Gentiles uncircumcised. Slaves should not worry about being slaves, and freedmen need not become slaves again. Verse 24 sums it up—walk before God in the calling you were in when the gospel called you. What matters is keeping the commands of God (1 Cor. 7:19).

This passage talks about position, not place, but the principle applies. As a general rule, stay where you were when you got saved. Bloom where you are planted.

That does not mean that you cannot change your situation. Paul says that if you can improve your status by becoming free, do it (1 Cor. 7:21). Therefore, you're not prohibited if you can improve your situation.

Does God tell believers to go to a particular place or do a certain thing? There are cases in the Bible of God putting a person in a specific place. He *told* Abraham to go to Canaan (Gen. 12:1-3). He *told* Jonah to go to Nineveh (Jonah 1:2). He *told* Philip to go to the desert (Acts 8:26). He *told* Peter to go to the house of Cornelius (Acts 10:17-20). He *told* Paul to go to Macedonia (Acts 16:10). In each of those cases, God communicated directly by *an audible voice* (see "The LORD had said to Abram" in Gen. 12:1; "the word of the LORD came to Jonah" in Jonah 1:1; "Now an angel of the Lord spoke to Philip" in Acts 8:26) or by *a vision and words* (see "While Peter thought about the vision, the Spirit said to him" in Acts 10:19 and "And a vision appeared to Paul in the night. A man of Macedonia stood and pleaded with him, saying, 'Come over to Macedonia and help us'" in Acts 16:9).

In those cases, God revealed His will through an audible voice, the appearance of an angel, or a vision that included an audible voice. (Based on the way the Spirit communicated to people in the book of Acts, it is safe to assume when the text says, "the Holy Spirit forbade them to preach the word in Asia" in Acts 16:6 and, "After they had come to Mysia, they tried to go into Bithynia, but the Spirit did not permit them" in Acts 16:7, the Holy Spirit spoke to them in an audible voice.) Notice carefully that all examples of individual guidance are instances of supernatural revelation. In his book *Decision Making and the Will of God: A Biblical Alternative to the Traditional View*, Garry Friesen concludes, "One could argue that God *may* give a believer guidance that is more specific than that found in the Bible. But if He does, it would be through supernatural means" (Friesen, p. 91, italics his).

The question is, "Are these cases of normal Christian experience, or are they unique experiences that are highly unusual?" "The examples of detailed divine guidance in Scripture are infrequent in appearance, limited in scope, and directed to persons who play a special role in the outworking of God's program on earth" (Friesen, p. 91). Furthermore, there are no examples in Scripture of God giving special instructions on the ordinary decisions of life. Therefore, the examples of direct communication in the Bible are the exceptions, not the rule. To illustrate, God once spoke through a donkey (Num. 22:28-30). As one author has suggested, "Should each believer keep [a donkey] in his backyard just in case?" (Friesen, p. 89).

Providence God does not work that way today, but He is in control of everything that happens and provides people with a particular place at a specific time for a particular purpose. He *providentially* put Esther in a place and position where she could save her people. In the providence of God, Esther was chosen queen and Mordecai discovered a plot to assassinate the king and another plot to eradicate the Jewish people. The point of the book of Esther is that God is working to provide for, protect, and preserve His people (Esther 4:14). The problem is that the Bible does not tell us how to interpret providence ahead of time. We usually look back and see providence.

To sum up, the personal will of God is for believers to serve the Lord according to their spiritual gifts, possibly to suffer, and perhaps to be providentially put in a particular place.

The Particular Will of God

In my experience, when believers ask about the will of God, they are usually concerned about a *particular* decision they have to make, such as whom to marry, which college to go to, which job to take, or where to live. Does God have a particular will regarding your marriage, college, vocation, etc.? Is there one specific person God has picked out for you to marry? Does God have a particular occupation for you to enter? Does God have an ideal plan uniquely designed in every detail of a person's life?

Marriage Does God have one and only one person picked out for you to marry? There are only two cases in the Bible where God determined who a person should marry. God created Eve for Adam. Adam had no choice. God chose Rebecca for Isaac. Isaac could have married someone else, but if he had done so, he would not have married the person God intended for him to marry.

The question is, "Are these normative or special cases?" The answer is that these are exceptional cases. There are no other such cases in the Bible. Furthermore, Paul says, "A wife is bound by the law as long as her husband lives; but if her husband dies, she is at liberty to be married to whom she wishes, only in the Lord" (1 Cor. 7:39). The only restriction Paul puts on the remarriage of a believing widow is that she marry a believer. You are free to marry any believer you want to marry!

There is freedom within the revealed will of God. In areas where the Bible does not give a command or principle, believers are free to choose their course of action.

Occupation Does the will of God include your vocation? In that, every individual has a spiritual gift and a natural talent, in a sense, God intends for a person to have a certain vocation. On the other hand, the Scripture never makes vocation a part of the will of God; instead, it says, "Whatever your hand finds to do, do *it* with your might; for *there is* no work or device or knowledge or wisdom in the grave where you are going" (Eccl. 9:10).

Location Does the will of God include your location? As mentioned, as a general rule, remain where you were when you were saved. If you can improve yourself, do it. There is freedom in the will of God. God is more interested in *who* you are than *where* you are. Friesen says, "The idea of an individual will of God for every detail of a person's life is not found in Scripture" (Friesen, pp. 82-83). "God does not have an ideal, detailed life plan uniquely designed for each believer that must be discovered in order to make correct decisions" (Friesen, p. 145).

In the final analysis, there is freedom in the will of God. The will of God is revealed in the Word of God. We are to obey His commands, the sum of which is to love one another. God has a will for our spiritual lives and, within His will, there is a great deal of freedom of choice in areas such as marriage, vocation, and location.

There is a difference between *determining the will of God* and *making decisions*. Determining the will of God is easy. Read the Bible. Once within the will of God, making decisions can be difficult. Here are some guidelines.

Pray Ask God for wisdom. James says, "If any of you lacks wisdom, let him ask of God, who gives to all liberally and without reproach, and it will be given to him" (Jas. 1:5). You can marry any Christian, but not every Christian will make a good mate for you. So, ask God for wisdom.

Seek Wise Counsel Seeking counselors (plural) is mentioned four times in Proverbs (Prov. 11:14; 15:22; 20:18; 24:6). The Bible speaks about wise, sensible spiritual leaders who ought to be able to give wise counsel to others. God told Moses, "Choose wise, understanding, and knowledgeable men from among your tribes, and I will make them heads over you" (Deut. 1:13). Then God told these judges, "Hear *the cases* between your brethren and judge righteously between a man and his brother or the stranger who is with him" (Deut. 1:16). Paul told the Corinthians, "I say this to your shame. Is it so, that there is not a wise man among you, not even one, who will be able to judge between his brethren?" (1 Cor. 6:5).

Spiritual decision-makers in the New Testament are to be "sober-minded" (1 Tim. 3:2; Titus 1:8). The Greek word translated "sober-minded" means "of sound mind, sane, sensible." It describes a person of balanced judgment.

Make a Wise Discussion Notice the way the apostles made some decisions. "Then the twelve summoned the multitude of the disciples and said, '*It is not desirable* that we should leave the Word of God and serve tables. Therefore, brethren, seek out from among you seven men of *good* reputation, full of the Holy Spirit and wisdom, whom we may appoint over this business'" (Acts 6:2-3, italics added). "They analyzed the problem, reviewed their assignments, and came up with a wise, practical plan that would meet all the relevant needs" (Friesen, p. 185).

"Therefore, when we could no longer endure it, *we thought it good* to be left in Athens alone, and sent Timothy, our brother and minister of God, and our fellow laborer in the gospel of Christ, to establish you and encourage you concerning your faith, that no one should be shaken by these afflictions; for you yourselves know that we are appointed to this" (1 Thess. 3:1-3, italics added).

"But I trust in the Lord that I myself shall also come shortly. Yet *I considered it necessary* to send to you Epaphroditus, my brother, fellow worker, and fellow soldier, but your messenger and the one who ministered to my need since he was longing for you all and was distressed because you had heard that he was sick" (Phil. 2:24-26, italics added).

"And when I come, whomever you approve by *your* letters I will send to bear your gift to Jerusalem. But *if it is fitting* that I go also, they will go with me" (1 Cor. 16:3-4, italics added). "He was simply calculating how it made the best use of his time and energy for the Lord" (Friesen, p. 184). The apostles made their decisions based on what was desirable, good, necessary, and fitting.

In some situations, unbelievers can be a valuable source of wisdom (Lk. 16:8).

In 1 Corinthians chapter 7, Paul tells a widow she is free to marry whomsoever she wills, but in his opinion, she is happier if she remains single (1 Cor. 7:40). In other words, it is undoubtedly a measure of the greatness of God's love that the matter of one's happiness is permitted as a valid consideration in the decision-making process. Obviously, it is not the only consideration, nor is it the primary factor (Mt. 6:19-33), but one's experience of happiness is certainly significant and should not be discounted in the decision-making process.

By the way, common sense is a part of wisdom. Use your common sense. In an article published in *Discipleship Journal*, Elaine Brown asks us to consider the following seven questions before saying "yes" to a new opportunity.

1. Will my spouse and children be adversely affected if I say "yes" to this?

2. Is this new opportunity likely to place undue stress on my mind, emotions, and/or body?

3. Am I fully aware of all that is involved in this commitment?

4. Could this new opportunity undermine my effectiveness in already existing commitments?

5. Will this opportunity enable me to use my God-given spiritual gifts and natural talents?

6. Would it be better for someone else to do this?

7. What are my motives for considering this opportunity?
    (Brown, cited by Ron Barnes, "Cultivating a Humble Heart," *Kindred Spirit*, vol. 22, No. 3, Autumn, 1998, p. 7).

Summary: Within God's revealed will in His Word and His providential placement, there is freedom for you to choose your course of action, even in the areas of marriage, occupation, and location, so make wise decisions.

Let's review. The *perfect* will of God is revealed in the Word of God. God's will is that you be transformed into the image of Christ. The *personal* will of God is that you serve Him and perhaps suffer and be placed in a particular place, but the suffering is not revealed ahead of time, and the placement is done providentially. When it comes to particulars, such as marriage and occupation, there is freedom for you to choose your course of action and still be in the will of God.

The Bible does not teach that God has an ideal will, He reveals it through inward impulses and outward signs. Within the revealed will of God, you have the freedom to make wise decisions.

On that blank page in the back of your Bible, under "Basics," write "9. The Will of God," and after that, "Romans 12:1-3."

Adam was hungry. He had had a long, challenging day naming animals. As the sun began to set, Adam discovered he had worked up an appetite. "I think we should eat," he said to Eve. "Let's call the evening meal 'supper.'" "Oh, you're so decisive, Adam," replied Eve admiringly. "I like that in a man. And 'supper' has a nice ring to it."

As they discussed how to proceed, they decided that Adam would gather fruit from the garden, and Eve would prepare it for their meal. Adam set about his task and soon returned with a basket full of ripe fruit. He gave it to Eve and went to soak his feet in the soothing current of the Pishon River until supper was ready.

He had been reviewing the animals' names for about five minutes when he heard his wife's troubled voice.

"Adam, could you help me for a moment?"

"What seems to be the problem, dear?" he replied.

"I'm not sure which of these lovely fruits I should prepare for supper. I've prayed for guidance from the Lord, but I'm not really sure what He wants me to do. I don't want to miss His will on my first decision. Would you go to the Lord and ask Him what I should do about supper?"

Adam's hunger intensifies, but he understands Eve's dilemma. So he left her to go speak with the Lord. Shortly, he returned. He appeared perplexed.

"Well?" probed Eve.

"He didn't really answer your question," he answered.

"What do you mean? Didn't He say anything?"

"Oh yes," replied Adam. "But He just repeated what He said earlier today during the garden tour: 'From any tree of the garden you may eat freely, but from the tree of the knowledge of good and evil you shall not eat.' I assure you, Eve, I steered clear of the forbidden tree."

"But that doesn't solve my problem," said Eve. "What should I prepare for tonight?"

From the rumbling in his stomach, Adam discovered that lions and tigers are not the only things that growl. So he said, "I've never seen such crisp, juicy apples. I feel a sense of peace about them. Why don't you prepare them for supper? Maybe while you're getting them ready, you'll experience the same peace I have."

"All right, Adam," she agreed. "I guess you've had more experience making decisions than 1. I appreciate your leadership. I'll call you when supper is ready."

"OK," replied Adam, relieved. "I'll get back to my easy bank." Adam was only halfway to the river when he heard Eve's call. He was so hungry that he jogged back to the clearing where she was working. But his anticipation evaporated when he saw her face.

"More problems?" he asked.

"Adam, I just can't decide what to do with these apples. I could slice, dice, mash, and bake them in a pie, a cobbler, fritters, or dumplings. Or we could just polish them and eat them raw. I really want to be your helper, but I also want to be certain of the Lord's will in this decision. Would you be a dear and go just one more time to the Lord with my problem?"

Since he didn't have any better solution himself, Adam did as Eve requested.

When he returned, he said, "I got the same answer as before: 'From *any* tree of the garden you may eat *freely;* but from the tree of the knowledge of good and evil you shall not eat.' "

Adam and Eve were both silent for a moment. Then Adam said, "You know, Eve, the Lord made that statement as though it ought to answer my question fully. I'm sure He could have told me what to eat and how to eat it, but I think He wants us to make those decisions. It was the same way with the animals today. He just left their names up to me."

Eve was incredulous. "Do you mean it doesn't matter which fruits we have for supper? Are you telling me I *can't* miss God's will in this decision?"

Adam explained: "The only way you could do that is to pick some fruit from the forbidden tree. But all of these fruits are all right. Why, I suppose we could eat all of them." Adam snapped his fingers and exclaimed, "Say, that's a great idea! Let's have fruit salad for supper!"

Eve hesitated. "What's a salad?"

(edited from Friesen, pp. 165-167).

Chapter 10

SPIRITUAL BASICS: THE PROVISION OF GOD

God created you so that you could have relationships. Relationships come in different shapes and sizes. A person can be a son or daughter, a brother or sister, a student and friend, an employee or employer, a husband or wife, a father or mother, etc. We were also designed to have a relationship with God. What word would you use to describe your relationship with the Lord? What does the relationship look like? A number of different words are used to describe our relationship with the Lord. Let's focus on three.

Provider

Abraham In Genesis 22, the Lord told Abraham to offer his son, Isaac, as a burnt offering (Gen. 22:1-2). When he got to the place for the burnt offering, "Then Abraham looked at his eyes and there behind him was the ram caught in the thicket by his horns so Abraham went and took the ram and offered it up for a burnt offering instead of his son. And Abraham called the name of the place, The-LORD-Will-Provide; as it is said to this day, 'In the Mount of the LORD it shall be provided" (Gen. 22:13-14). Abraham named the place "The-Lord-Will-Provide" and Moses adds the editorial note that there was a proverbial saying to his day that "In the Mount of the Lord it shall be provided."

This passage proclaims and illustrates that the Lord will provide a sacrifice to be a substitute. Jesus Christ is the Lamb of God who takes away the sin of the world (Jn. 1:29). Paul alludes to this passage in Romans 8:32, which says, "He who did not spare His own Son, but delivered Him up for us all, how shall He not with Him also give us all things?" The word translated "spared" in is a verb from the same root as the one used in the Greek translation of Genesis (the Septuagint) for "provide" (Ross).

"The Lord-Will-Provide" (Jehovah-Jireh) is one of the names of God in the book of Genesis. It indicates that He will provide a substitute sacrifice and that the Lord is a provider for His people. He provides salvation for sin, life for death, strength for weakness, joy for sorrow, and heaven instead of hell. Do you know Him as your provider?

Israel "Therefore say to the children of Israel: 'I *am* the LORD; **I will** bring you out from under the burdens of the Egyptians, **I will** rescue you from their bondage, and **I will** redeem you with an outstretched arm and with great judgments. **I will** take you as My people, and **I will** be your God. Then you shall know that I *am* the LORD your God who brings you out from under the burdens of the Egyptians. **And I will** bring you into the land which I swore to give to Abraham, Isaac, and Jacob; and **I will** give it to you *as* a heritage: I *am* the LORD" (Ex. 6:6-8, bold type added). The Lord says "I will" seven times in these three verses. These are the seven things that he will provide for them. These seven things are summarized in Leviticus. "I am the LORD your God, who brought you out of the land of Egypt, to give you the land of Canaan and to be your God" (Lev. 25:38). So, in short, God told Israel he wanted to redeem them (Ex. 6:6), be their God (Ex. 6:7), and give them the land of Canaan (Ex. 6:8). These are some of the things the Lord will provide for them.

They no sooner got out of Egypt than they began to complain (Ex. 16:2). Their complaint was that in Egypt they had "pots of meat" and bread to eat "to the full," but Moses brought us to the wilderness to kill us with starvation (Ex. 16:3). In response, the Lord said, "I will rain bread from heaven" (Ex. 16:4). In fact, He provided "meat to eat in the evening and in the morning bread to the full" (Ex. 16:8).

Speaking to the Lord, David says in Psalm 65, "You visit the earth and water it, You greatly enrich it; the river of God is full of water; You provide their grain, for so You have prepared it" (Ps. 65:9). With rain provided by God, the earth is enriched, rivers are full, and grains grow. We give thanks before we eat because we recognize that God has provided the food.

Believers God is still in the business of redeeming people. Paul says in Christ, "We have redemption through His blood, the forgiveness of sins" (Col. 1:14). In other words, because Christ died for our sins and rose from the dead (1 Cor. 15:3), those who trust in a forgiven of their sins and become the children of God (Jn. 1:12). Moreover, "He who did not spare His own Son but delivered Him up for us all, how shall He not with Him also give us all things?"(Rom. 8:32).

Shepherd

"The LORD *is* my shepherd. I shall not want" (Ps. 23:1). David "had been a shepherd of sheep as a youth and later became a shepherd of God's people as their king" (Constable). In this poem, he reverses roles, saying that the Lord is his Shepard and he is a lamb.

David watched over, provided greener pastures, found water, and guarded the flock so he felt God would provide for and watch over him. As his shepherd, the Lord meets all of David's needs so well that he can say, "I shall not want." The theme and, for that matter, the idea of the whole psalm is contained in the statement, "I shall not want" (Alexander). "These words are the keystone of the Psalm" (Perowne). "This is the main idea in the psalm" (Barnes). "As David's shepherd, the Lord provided all David needed" (Constable). The shepherd meets various needs. What are those needs?

Physical "He makes me to lie down in green pastures" (Ps. 23:2a). The reference to "green pasture" suggests that David is speaking of God meeting his physical need for food. If "green pastures" refers to physical food, lying down in a green pasture is a picture of abundant supply. The sheep is not only fed; he is full, "fully fed" or "satisfied" (Barnes). Furthermore, the shepherd makes the small lamb lie down in green pastures (plural), which indicates that this abundant supply is not an isolated incident but a reoccurring event.

"He leads me beside the still waters" (Ps. 23:2b). The Lord leads to "still" waters. Because of the heat and dryness of the climate, sheep require water daily. The sheep were frightened by rapidly moving water. So the shepherd "stilled" the water.

Spiritual "He restores my soul" (Ps. 23:3a). Sheep tend to wander away from the flock. Like sheep, believers, too, tend to wander away. As the songwriter says, "Prone to wander, Lord I feel it; prone to leave the God I love." The shepherd leaves the ninety-nine to find and restore the wandering one.

"He leads me in the paths of righteousness for His name's sake" (Ps. 23:3b). After the Lord restores us, He wants to lead us so that we do not wander off again. The Shepherd guides the sheep in a path of righteousness.

Emotional "Yea, though I walk through the valley of the shadow of death, I will fear no evil" (Ps. 23:4a). The Hebrew word translated "shadow of death" means "deep shadow" and is used figuratively of distress or extreme danger. Valley, or rather "deep cliff" or "ravine," made the shadow grow deeper and more chilling as the sun sank. The expression "the shadow of death" signifies the most fearful darkness, such as Hades (Job 10:21), the shaft of a mine (Job 28:3), or the darkness that makes itself felt in a wild, uninhabited desert (Jer. 2:6; Delitzsch). There is an allusion to the dread of the darkness of sheep.

"For You *are* with me; Your rod and Your staff, they comfort me" (Ps. 23:4b). "The shepherd's rod (a cudgel worn at the belt) beat off attacking animals, and his staff (walking stick) kept the sheep away from physical dangers such as precipices. Likewise,

God comes to the defense of His people when our spiritual enemies attack us. "The promises of the Lord's presence assure us of His protection in times of danger when we fear (Matt. 28:20; Heb. 13:5)" (Constable).

"You prepare a table before me in the presence of my enemies" (Ps. 23:5a). The shepherd prepares a table, a place of peace and fellowship, in the very presence of the sheep's enemies. The enemies watch quietly without being able to do anything (Delitzsch).

"You anoint my head with oil; my cup runs over" (Ps. 23:5b). The shepherd anoints the head of the sheep with oil, which was used to prevent rodents from harming the sheep. "David's "cup" symbolized his lot in life that overflowed with abundant blessings.

"Surely goodness and mercy shall follow me all the days of my life" (Ps. 23:6a). Goodness and mercy would pursue him throughout his life. To follow here does not mean to bring up the rear but to pursue vigorously (Ps. 83:15; Kidner).

Eternal "And I will dwell in the house of the LORD forever" (Ps. 23:6b). "Dwelling in the LORD's 'house' (i.e., the sanctuary in Jerusalem) was a picture of enjoying full communion and fellowship with the Lord. "'Forever' translates a Hebrew phrase (*'orek yamim*, lit. 'length of days'), which, when used elsewhere of men, usually refers to a lengthy period of time (such as one's lifetime), not eternity (cf. Deut. 30:20; Job 12:12; Ps. 91:16; Prov. 3:2, 16; Lam. 5:20).... While the psalmist may not have been speaking specifically of an afterlife in God's presence, in the progress of revelation his words come to express such a hope for God's people, who now understand the full ramifications of the psalm's affirmation that God protects His own. In the same way, the statements in Psalms 17:15, 49:15, and 73:24 become, on the lips of a Christian, a testimony of faith in God's final vindication of the righteous, even beyond the grave" (Chisholm, "A Theology ....," pp. 287, 288, cited by Constable).

Jesus is the Shepherd (Isa. 40:11 says the Messiah is a shepherd). He is the Good Shepherd (Jn. 10:11), the Great Shepherd (Heb. 13:20), and the Chief Shepherd (1 Pet. 5:4). The Shepherd does this by dying for the sheep (Jn. 10:11). In the Old Testament, the sheep died for the shepherd, but in the New Testament, the Shepherd died for the sheep (Wiersbe on 1 Peter 2).

To sum up, when the Lord is your shepherd, He meets your physical, spiritual, emotional, and eternal needs.

David says, "The Lord is *my* shepherd." For this to work, the Lord must be *your* shepherd. Make Him your shepherd; take all your needs to Him (1 Pet. 5:7). "Everything, therefore, hinges on the personal pronoun *my*. Unless He is *my* Shepherd, then the rest of the psalm does not belong to me" (MacDonald; italics his).

Father

The Lord's Prayer "In this manner, therefore, pray: Our Father in heaven, hallowed be Your name" (Mt. 6:9). Jesus says to pray "in this manner," not "in these words" (Plummer; Wiersbe). God is to be addressed as "our Father." Jesus came to reveal the Father. "No one has seen God at any time. The only begotten Son, who was in the bosom of the Father, he has declared Him" (Jn. 1:18).

Addressing God as Father means that this prayer is not to be prayed by everyone because God is not the Father of everybody. This prayer is for those who have trusted Jesus Christ for eternal life and, thus, become the children of God.

The first petition concerning God is that His name is to be "hallowed." The idea is to venerate, reverence. We are not to begin with our wants, not even with ourselves; we are to begin with God. The second petition concerning God is "Your kingdom come" (Mt. 6:10a). This request is "clearly eschatological" (Toussaint). The third petition concerning God is "Your will be done on earth as it is in heaven" (Mt. 6:10b). Most people pray to get their will done in heaven as it in on earth. The purpose of prayer is to get God's will done on earth.

The first petition concerning us is that we ask God, "Give us this day our daily bread" (Mt. 6:11). This is a request for our physical provisions. In the wilderness, God supplied the Israelites with bread daily (Ex. 16:4). I once heard an older man say that he had prayed this prayer every day for decades and he had never lacked for his daily provisions. He attributed that to God's answer to this prayer.

The second petition concerning us is "And forgive us our debts, as we forgive our debtors" (Mt. 6:12). Jesus moves from physical needs to spiritual needs. The first spiritual need is the need for pardon. Sins are viewed as debts to God that need to be wiped away. The debt of sin is forgiven under two conditions: confession (6:12; 1 Jn. 1:9) and a forgiving spirit (Mt. 6:12). The petition, "forgive us our debts" is "confession" and the phrase "as we forgive our debtors" means that we should "cultivate a spirit of forgiveness" (Plummer; Tasker; Wiersbe). The point here is that part of prayer is being forgiven and forgiving.

The third petition concerning us is "and do not lead us into temptation, but deliver us from the evil one" (Mt. 6:13a). This need is for protection. The Greek word translated "temptation" means "trial" and "temptation." Some take this to be a trial, even the trial that is to come in the future. Others take it to be a reference to temptation. So, what is the meaning of "temptation" in this passage? The two requests, "Do not lead us into temptation" and "Deliver us from the evil one," are connected by "but," which in Greek is a word of strong contrast. Therefore, since being delivered from the evil one is in contrast to not being led into temptation, the word rendered "temptation" means temptation. The two parts interpret each other (Alexander; see also Walvoord).

Barclay suggests that asking for daily bread is our need in the present, that asking for forgiveness deals with our past, and that asking not to be tempted is about the future. He concludes, "In these pure brief petitions, we are taught to lay the present, the past, and the future before the footstool of the grace of God." Barclay also suggests that this prayer brings the whole of life before the whole of God. Our need for bread concerns God the Father, the Sustainer of all life. Our need for forgiveness is related to Jesus Christ, the Savior and our need to overcome temptation involves the Holy Spirit, the Strengthener. He concludes, "Jesus teaches us to bring the whole of life to the whole of God, and to bring the whole of God to the whole of life."

The Lord's Sermon "Therefore, I say to you, do not worry about your life, what you will eat or what you will drink; nor about your body, what you will put on. Is not life more than food and the body more than clothing? Look at the birds of the air, for they neither sow nor reap nor gather into barns; yet your heavenly Father feeds them. Are you not of more value than they? Which of you by worrying can add one cubit to his stature? So why do you worry about clothing? Consider the lilies of the field, how they grow: they neither toil nor spin; and yet I say to you that even Solomon in all his glory was not arrayed like one of these. Now if God so clothes the grass of the field, which today is, and tomorrow is thrown into the oven, will He not much more clothe you, O you of little faith? Therefore do not worry, saying, 'What shall we eat?' or 'What shall we drink?' or 'What shall we wear?' For after all these things the Gentiles seek. For your heavenly Father knows that you need all these things. But seek first the kingdom of God and His righteousness, and all these things shall be added to you. Therefore, do not worry about tomorrow, for tomorrow will worry about its own things. Sufficient for the day is its own trouble" (Mt. 6:25-34).

That does not mean that God delivers the food to our doorstep like Uber Eats. He supplies this need through our work. Paul said, "If anyone will not work, neither shall he eat" (2 Thess. 3:10).

Paul "Now you Philippians know also that in the beginning of the gospel, when I departed from Macedonia, no church shared with me concerning giving and receiving but you only. For even in Thessalonica, you sent *aid* once and again for my necessities. Not that I seek the gift, but I seek the fruit that abounds to your account. Indeed, I have all and abound. I am full, having received from Epaphroditus the things *sent* from you, a sweet-smelling aroma, an acceptable sacrifice, well pleasing to God. And my God shall supply all your need according to His riches in glory by Christ Jesus" (Phil. 4:15-19).

Peter "Therefore humble yourselves under the mighty hand of God, that He may exalt you in due time, casting all your care upon Him, for He cares for you" (1 Pet. 5:6-7).

Summary: As Provider, Shepherd, and Father, God wants to supply our needs as we depend upon Him.

On that blank page in the back of your Bible, under "Basics," write "10. Provision of God," and after that, "Philippians 4:19."

In the stock market crash of 1929, J. C. Penney's dry goods business was financially secure, but he had made some unwise personal commitments that troubled him deeply. A combination of circumstances had so completely broken him physically and mentally that he had to be hospitalized. He was so overwhelmed with the fear of death that one night, in his room, Mr. Penney wrote farewell letters to his wife and son, for he did not expect to live through the night. The next morning, he awakened and heard singing in the hospital chapel near his room. He pulled himself together and slipped into the chapel as the congregation began to sing, "God will take care of you."

"Suddenly, something happened," J. C. Penney recalled many years later. "I can't explain it. I can only call it a miracle. I felt as if

I had been instantly lifted out of the darkness of a dungeon into warm, brilliant sunlight. I felt as if I had been transported from hell to paradise. I felt the power of God as I had never felt it before. I am now 71, and my life has been worry-free since that glorious moment in the chapel when I really heard, "God will take care of you."

Chapter 11

SPIRITUAL BASICS: THE LOVE OF GOD

One of the Bible's most basic, important, and significant spiritual truths is love. "And now abide faith, hope, love, these three; but the greatest of these *is* love" (1 Cor. 13:13). What does the Bible say about love?

God's Love Is Sacrificial

There are four Greek words for love. Eros means "love, romantic love, or sexual passion." It is not used in the New Testament in any form.

Storge means "love, affection, especially of parents and children." In ancient writings, it is rarely used, and when it is, it is almost exclusively used to describe family relationships. It may also represent a love of country or enthusiasm for a favorite sports team. It is not used in the New Testament by itself, but a compound form appears in Romans 12:10, where it is translated "brotherly love." In other words, true love (Rom. 12:9) looks at believers with affectionate regard (Rom. 12:10) because believers are members of the same family (Rom. 12:10).

Philia means "love, a strong friendship." It is love with emotion. In Titus 1:4, wives are told to love their husbands and children. Lenski says that "phileo" denotes mere affection, romantic attachment, or passion (see his comment on Eph. 5:25). Young women need to be admonished to be affectionate. Men need affection more than sex. A man can live without sex; it is more challenging to live without warmth and affection.

Agape means "doing what is best; seeking their highest good." It is an act of the will whereby one chooses to do what is best for the one loved. Jesus used this word for love when He said, "Love your enemies" (Mt. 5:44). You don't have to like them, but in any relationship with them, you seek their highest good. This is also the word used for God's love for us, our love for God, and our love for one another (see William Barclay, *More New Testament Words*, pp. 11-15).

When the Bible says God loves us, it uses the Greek word that indicates He seeks our highest good; He does what is best for us. There is another element to God's love for us that is not embedded in the meaning of the word agape but is indicated by its usage. "But God demonstrates His own love toward us, in that while we were still sinners, Christ died for us" (Rom. 5:8). In other words, God's love is also sacrificial.

God's love is Everlasting

The Question "Who shall separate us from the love of Christ" (Rom. 8:35a). The expression "the love of Christ" refers to Christ's love for us, not our love for Christ (Godet; Sandy and Headlam; Hodge). The question is "who," not "what," but the following list consists of things, not people. Paul is personifying these things.

Paul asks, "Shall tribulation or distress, or persecution, or famine or nakedness, or peril or sword" (Rom. 8:35b). Tribulation is a Greek word that means "pressure." It is used figuratively of tribulation and affliction. The Greek word rendered "distress" means "narrowness of space, difficulty, distress." Persecution, famine, and nakedness are self-evident. A peril is a danger; a sword refers to a life-threatening situation, such as death. Except for the last one, Paul has already experienced all of these in his lifetime (2 Cor. 11). These seven sufferings are listed to cover the full range of experiences that seem to pose a challenge to the reality of Christ's love for us, but going through any of these, believers are tempted to ask, "Does God still love me?"

Paul adds, "As it is written for your sake, we are killed all the day long. We are counted as sheep for the slaughter" (Rom. 8:36). This quotation from Psalm 44:22 demonstrates that trials and tribulations are not new. God's people have always had to face them. They who love God (Ps. 44:17-21; Rom. 8:28) have always had to face death daily. Psalm 44:22 also refers to a more severe trial. A sentence of death has been pronounced but not yet executed. It hangs over their heads (Godet). They are like sheep chosen for slaughter but are not yet killed.

The Answer Paul's response is, "Yet in all these things we are more than conquerors through Him that loved us" (Rom. 8:37). These things not only do not separate us from Christ's love, but they make us more than conquerors by forcing us to depend even more on Him who loved us. We have enough power through Christ to conquer and still have strength besides. Perhaps being more than a conqueror refers to the joint-heirship with Jesus Christ (Rom. 8:17). Trials do not conquer us; we conquer them and then some. We do not just conquer trials; we triumph because of them.

In John Milton's *Paradise Lost*, Satan says, "Who overcomes by force, hath overcome but half his foe." Satan says this line while reflecting on his expulsion from heaven and his plans to use trickery and craftiness instead of force to thwart God's plans.

Therefore, Paul could personally conclude, "For I am persuaded that neither death nor life nor angels nor principalities nor powers nor things present nor things to come nor height nor depth nor any other created thing should be able to separate us from the love of God which is in Christ Jesus, our Lord" (Rom. 8:38-39). Paul was personally persuaded that nothing, absolutely nothing, could separate believers from God's love. No condemnation, neither death nor life can. Death is, no doubt, mentioned first because of the reference to death in the psalm just quoted (Rom. 8:36). In the Old Testament, death was the dreaded separator of loved ones and even possibly the separator of people from God's fellowship (Ps. 6:5, 39; 88:5, except verse 4), but for Paul to die was to be "with Christ," which was far better than life (2 Cor. 5:8; Phil. 1:21-23). Life includes interests, enticements, distractions, seductions, and distresses (14:8-9).

No creature like an angel, principality, or power can. Principalities and powers can denote civil authorities, but coupled with angels, they can also be angelic hierarchy categories (Sandy and Headlam). Neither angels nor demons can separate us from the love of God. Not demons, because Christ has once and for all won the decisive battle over them (Col. 2:15; Eph. 1:21, 22; 1 Pet. 3:22). J. P. Phillips said, "Remember the powers that we assume will be the powers that have been." No circumstance, either now or later, actual or potential, can. These possibilities include events, experiences, and even emotions we feel. As Shakespeare said, "Past and to come seems best. Things present worst" (Shakespeare, *King Henry IV*).

No conceivable location, neither the highest height nor the deepest depth, can separate a believer from God's love. Neither the highest point—Mt. Everest—nor the lowest point on the face of the earth, which is thirteen hundred feet below sea level at the Dead Sea, can separate one from the love of God. Perhaps this refers to heaven or hell (Ps. 139:8). If so, this verse is hyperbole because believers cannot go to hell. The point is that nothing in heaven or on earth (Hodge; or perhaps in hell) can separate believers from God's love. No other conceivable thing, no created thing, can. Anything not contemplated by the preceding cannot interfere or intervene between us and divine love for us.

The unfailing love of God is greater than anything conceivable. This love is "in Christ Jesus, our Lord." To be in Christ is to be in God's love. Nothing can change that, but only those who love God (Rom. 8:28) and, thus, obey Him (Jn. 14:15) will fully realize and appreciate it (Eph. 3:14-19) and abide in it (Jn. 15:10).

Charles Haddon Spurgeon, the famous British Baptist preacher of the 19th century, and a friend were walking down a country lane when Spurgeon noticed a sign on top of a weather vane that read, "God is love." Spurgeon remarked to his companion that he thought a weather vane inappropriate for such a message since weather vanes are changeable and God's love is not. The friend disagreed, suggesting, "You misconstrue the meaning. That weather vane tells us that God is love whichever way the wind blows."

To sum up, nothing, no condition, creature, circumstance, or conceivable location, or anything else, can change God's love for us.

Think about it. Nothing can separate you from God or His love. Nothing—ever—not in time or eternity. Ruth Harms Calkin has paraphrased this passage: "God, I may fall flat on my face and fail until I feel old and beaten and done in, but your love for me is changeless. All the music may go out of my life. My private world may shatter to dust. Even so, You will hold me in the palm of Your steady hand. No turn in the affairs of my fractured life can buffet you. Satan, with all of his braggadocio, can distract you. Nothing can separate me from your measureless love—pain can't, disappointment can't, anguish can't, yesterday, today, tomorrow can't, the loss of my dearest love can't, death can't, life can't, riots, war, insanity, hunger, neurosis, disease—none of these nor all of them heaped together can budge the fact that I am dearly loved and completely forgiven and forever free through Christ Jesus, Your beloved Son."

"And you have forgotten the exhortation which speaks to you as to sons: my son do not despise the chastening of the Lord, nor be discouraged when you are rebuked by Him; For whom the Lord loves he chastens and scourges every son He receives" (Heb. 12:5-6). The readers had forgotten an exhortation recorded in Proverb 3:11-12, a son should not despise the chastening of the Lord.

The Greek word translated "despise" means "to think lightly of" or "make light of" and the one rendered "chastening" is the word "training, discipline," which includes teaching and correction. Children of God should not take the child-rearing of God the Father lightly. Nor should they be discouraged (12:5; see 12:3) when God rebukes, that is, corrects them. The Greek word rendered "rebuke" means "to bring to light, expose, connect, convince, correct."

The reason (see "for" in 12:6) is that God loves, disciplines, and scourges every son. The Greek word translated "scourges" means "to whip or flag." Thus, Proverbs teaches that the divine discipline of a son is evidence of divine love. The readers have forgotten that. When trouble comes, we think, "God is displeased with me."

In the context of Hebrews, discipline at least includes persecution (Heb. 12:3-4). God does not directly cause persecution, but He does incorporate those kinds of circumstances in His training program because He loves His children (Rom. 8:28). Therefore, the believer should not "despair, compromise or apostatize in the face of persecution" (Kent). A surgeon said to a patient, "This may hurt you, but it will not injure you."

God's Love Is Unimaginable

Their Position Paul begins his prayer by saying, "For this reason, I bow my knees to the Father of our Lord Jesus Christ. From whom the whole family in heaven and earth is named that He would grant you, according to the riches of His glory, to be strengthened with might through His Spirit in the inner man" (Eph. 3:14-16). This prayer is for power. Paul piles one word onto another to emphasize the power he desires the believer to experience. "Strengthened with might" means "to wax strong with power." This power is to be in the inner man through the Holy Spirit. The standard by which Paul desires that this prayer be answered is the "riches of His glory."

The result of this prayer is that the inner man might be empowered by the Holy Spirit "that Christ may dwell in your hearts through faith" (Eph. 3:17a). The Greek word translated "dwell" means "to settle down and to be at home." Paul is not referring to the initial indwelling of Christ at the moment of regeneration. The idea is that Christ might be the center, the dominant factor, in the believer's life. There is a difference between being in a house and dwelling, that is, "feeling comfortable" in that house.

The believer's part is faith. As believers live by faith, that is, as they believe God's Word and trust Him for the enablement to do what God says in His Word, they are strengthened through the Holy Spirit, and Jesus Christ becomes more "at home" in them (Gal. 2:20; 4:19; 5:6).

The Purpose Paul gives the purpose for his petition. "That you, being rooted and grounded in love, may be able to comprehend with all the saints what is the width and length and depth and height—to know the love of Christ which passes knowledge" (Eph. 3:17b-19a). To communicate his point, Paul mixes metaphors from biology and architecture. Believers are to be rooted like a plant and grounded (Greek: "to lay the foundation") like a building in love. They are to be a well-rooted tree and a well-founded building regarding the virtue of love. Both of these figures convey the concept of being fixed, firmly established.

The purpose is being established in love, believers might be able to comprehend with all the saints what the width, length, depth, and height are to know the love of Christ, which passes knowledge. In other words, the purpose is that believers may comprehend the love of Christ.

Believers are to comprehend the width, length, depth, and height of the love of Christ. The width of His love is broad enough to include Jews and Gentiles in one body (Eph. 2:1-7; 13-17; Pentecost; Toussaint). The length of His love is from eternity to eternity (Eph. 1:4; 2:7; 3:11; Pentecost; Toussaint). The depth of His love extends to the depth of depravity where God's grace saves sinners (Eph. 2:1-3; 11, 12; Pentecost; Toussaint). The height of His love extends to the heavenlies, where God's grace places saved sinners (Eph. 1:3; 2:4-7).

This is the love Paul desires that believers know. Notice the paradoxical way he says it: "To know the love of Christ which passes knowledge." How can that be? The love of Christ is beyond the knowledge of the natural man and even the immature saint. It is as believers grow in love that they comprehend love.

To sum up, God can strengthen believers so that Christ will dwell in them and help them comprehend the love of Christ.

What child understands the extent of his parent's love? None. Not until the child becomes a parent does he or she understand that kind of love. Likewise, believers don't understand God's love until they grow in love. D. L. Moody used to say, "Columbus discovered America, but what did he know about its great lakes, rivers, forests, and the Mississippi River? He died without knowing much about what he had discovered. So many of us have discovered something of the love of God, but there are heights, depths, and lengths of which we do not know" (*Our Daily Bread*, 7/7/1958). How deep have you gone in the unfathomed ocean of God's love?

Summary: The love of God is sacrificial, everlasting, and unimaginable.

On that blank page in the back of your Bible, under "Basics," write "11. Love of God," and after that, "Eph. 3:17-19."

This chapter begins with the observation that one of the Bible's most basic, important, and significant spiritual truths is love. Love is one of the major messages of the Bible. Many consider the book of Romans the deepest book in the Bible. When you go to the deepest depths of Scripture, you find the love of God. Ephesians takes us to the highest heights, the heavenlies. When you reach the highest point of the Scripture, find the love of God.

Jesus said the great commandment is "You shall love the Lord your God with all your heart, with all your soul, and with all your mind ... and the second is like it: You shall love your neighbor as yourself" (Mt. 22:37-40). There are three great lessons here.

First, God loves us. God loves us with everlasting love. Jeremiah wrote, "The LORD has appeared of old to me, *saying:* "Yes, I have loved you with an everlasting love; Therefore with lovingkindness I have drawn you" (Jer. 31:3). D. L. Moody once said, "I know of no truth in the whole Bible that ought to come home to us with such power and tenderness is that of the love of God. Satan constantly tries to persuade men and women that the Lord does not love them. He succeeded in making our first parents believe that lie, and too often, he succeeds with us. We make a mistake when we tell our children that the heavenly Father does not love them when they do wrong but only when they do right. That is not taught in the Scripture. Because your child is fretful or has committed some act of disobedience, you do not cast them out as though he did not belong to you. So, when we go astray, it does not follow that God despises us. It's the sin that He hates" (*Our Daily Bread*, 9/20/1976; 11/24/1985).

Joseph was sold into slavery by his brothers, falsely accused by Potiphar's wife, and ended up in prison. Did God love him when He allowed his brothers to sell him into slavery? Did God love him when He allowed Potiphar's wife to falsely accuse him? Did God love him when He allowed him to end up in prison? Joseph thought so. After it was over, he said to his brothers, "You meant evil against me, but God meant it for good, in order to bring it about as it is this day, to save many people alive" (Gen. 50:19).

Second, we should love God. "Hear, O Israel: The LORD our God, the LORD is one. You shall love the LORD your God with all your heart, with all your soul, and with all your strength" (Dt. 6:4-5).

Third, we should love one another. "In this, the love of God was manifested toward us, that God has sent His only begotten Son into the world, that we might live through Him. In this is love, not that we loved God, but that He loved us and sent His Son to be the propitiation for our sins. Beloved, if God so loved us, we also ought to love one another" (1 Jn. 4:9-11). "A new commandment I give to you, that you love one another; as I have loved you, that you also love one another. By this, all will know that you are My disciples, if you have love for one another" (Jn. 13:34-35).

But our love for God and others begins with realizing how much God loves us. According to NASA, in the early 20th century, astronomers thought the Milky Way comprised everything in the universe and was thought to be 300,000 light-years across. In 1929, the universe was thought to be 280 million light-years across. In 1955, the size of the universe was recalibrated, and the conclusion was that it was 4 billion light years across. That estimate was revised in 1965 to be 25 billion light-years across. In 1993, the estimate was 30 billion light-years across and in 2006, the conclusion was that the universe is 94 billion light-years across (for this and more, see the article at https://imagine.gsfc.nasa.gov/educators/programs/cosmictimes/educators/guide/age_size.html).

To communicate to a child how much you love him or her, we stretch our arms out as far as we can and we say, "I love you this much." God says, "I love you this much and uses the universe as stretched-out arms."

Chapter 12

SPIRITUAL BASICS: THE JUDGMENT SEAT

In all of the New Testament, it is only mentioned twice—by name. Yet, as one fellow said to me once, it seems like it's on every other page of the New Testament. Evidently, it is a subject that many preachers never mention. I say that because of something that has happened to me. Since I have systematically gone through the New Testament book by book, I have been forced to talk about this subject. So, I have mentioned it fairly often. People tell me, "I never heard of the subject until I came to your church." What subject might that be? The Judgment Seat of Christ.

Because the Judgment Seat of Christ will be so significant in eternity, I consider it one of the Bible's most basic and important spiritual truths. It is significant in eternity because it is at the Judgment Seat of Christ that rewards are given and those rewards determine our place in the kingdom. So, what do we need to know about the Judgment Seat of Christ?

Everything will be Judged

Paul's Aim "We are confident, yes, well pleased rather to be absent from the body and to be present with the Lord. Therefore we make it our aim, whether present or absent, to be well pleasing to Him" (2 Cor. 5:8-9). Paul was confident and pleased that he would be present with the Lord when he was absent from the body. No matter where he was, whether in the body or out, Paul aimed to be well pleasing to the Lord.

Paul's Reason "For we must all appear before the judgment seat of Christ, that each one may receive the things done in the body, according to what he has done, whether good or bad" (2 Cor. 5:10). When Paul says "all" he means all believers. Unbelievers appear before the Great White Throne Judgment (Rev. 20:11-15). Believers eternal destiny will never be judged (Jn. 5:24).

Several words in verse 10 need to be explained. The Greek word translated "appear" means "to make visible, clear, known, manifest." Here, it could refer to nothing more than an appearance, like appearing in court before a judge. Or it could mean we must stand revealed in our true character (Hodge). Hughes says, "To be made manifest means not just to appear, but to be laid bare, stripped of every outward facade of respectability, and openly revealed in the full and true reality of one's character. All our hypocrisies and concealments, all our secret, intimate sins of thought and deed, will be open to the scrutiny of Christ."

Wow! Is Hughes reading something into this passage that is not there? Will our *thoughts*, as well as our deeds, be on display? Jesus said, "Every idle word men may speak, they will give an account of it in the day of judgment" (Mt. 12:36). That passage *may* be to unbelievers, but Jesus told His *disciples*, "For there is nothing covered, that will not be revealed, nor hidden that will not be known. Therefore, whatever you have spoken in the dark will be heard in the light, and what you have spoken in the ear in inner rooms will be proclaimed on the housetops" (Lk. 12:1-3). James says the words of believers will be judged (Jas. 3:1). Paul says, "Therefore, judge nothing before the time, until the Lord comes, who will both bring to light the hidden things of darkness and reveal the counsels of the hearts" (1 Cor. 4:5). The "counsels of the hearts" refers to motives. The Lord's judgment will consider all the facts, including motives. The writer to the Hebrews says, "There is no creature hidden from His sight, but all things are naked and open to the eyes of Him to whom *we* [believers] must give an account" (Heb. 4:13, italics added). All believers must give an account to the all-seeing, all-knowing God. Paul says that everything believers do in their bodies (in their lives) will be taken into consideration, both good and bad. In his book on rewards, Wall says, "Every thought, every word, every deed, and every motive will one day be evaluated by Jesus" (Wall, p. 12).

As a young Christian, I was taught that only our works would be considered at the Judgment Seat of Christ (1 Cor. 3:11-15). As an evangelist, I spent a week with a pastor who tried to convince me that everything good and evil would be considered at the Judgment Seat. To use Paul's expression, I withstood him to the face. I argued with him for one solid week. After leaving town, I thought, "He may have a point." Years later, after studying all the passages involved, I had to conclude that he was right and I was wrong.

So Don't Judge Other Believers

In Romans 14, Paul discusses the relationship between strong and weak believers. He begins by telling the strong to receive the weak (Rom. 14:1). The strong believed they could eat anything received with thanksgiving (1 Tim. 4:4-5). The weak were vegetarians (Rom. 14:2). Paul tells the strong not to despise the weak and the weak not to judge the strong (Rom. 14:3). Love dictates that believers are not to judge one another concerning amoral things because each believer is accountable to his master (Rom. 14:4).

The Question In developing a reason why Christians should not judge another believer, Paul asks a second question: "But why do you judge your brother? Or why do you show contempt for your brother?" (Rom. 14:10a). These two questions are addressed to two groups mentioned earlier: the strong and the weak. Paul asks, "Why do the weak judge the strong, and why do the strong show contempt for the weak?" Notice Paul uses the word "brother" in both questions. These are fellow believers judging and despising one another.

The Explanation "For we shall all stand before the judgment seat of Christ. For it is written: As I live, says the Lord, every knee shall bow to Me, and every tongue shall confess to God" (Rom. 14:10b-11). All believers must stand before the Judgment Seat of Christ. Paul affirms this truth by quoting Isaiah 14:23. God will judge all men. Paul is applying the universal truth to believers. Believers should not inappropriately judge others because the Lord is the judge.

Paul says, "So then each of us shall give account of himself to God. Therefore, let us not judge one another anymore, but rather resolve this, not to put a stumbling block or a cause to fall in our brother's way" (Rom. 14:12-13). Because God is the judge, we should not judge others, especially concerning amoral things. The word translated "resolve" is the same Greek word rendered "judge" in the first part of the verse. Paul is saying, 'Do not judge one another. If you want to judge, judge that you will not cause a brother to stumble. Do not pass judgment on your brother's decisions but on your own."

We are commanded to judge false doctrine (2 Cor. 11:4) and the difference between good and evil (1 Cor. 6:2-4). We are not to judge other believers concerning amoral things. In Paul's day, the amoral items he had in mind were food and festivals, diet and days. In our day, it goes from A to Z. The modern list includes alcohol, bingo, cosmetics, dancing, eating pork, football on Sunday, going to movies, Halloween, insurance, jeans, kissing, lodges, newspapers on Sunday, opera, pants, rock music, smoking, TV, wine, X-rated movies, and zippers instead of buttons. Paul teaches that we should not judge one another based on moral issues. We are to know that we all have to give an account of ourselves to the Lord.

Because we will all stand before the Judgment Seat of Christ, there are things we should not do. In this passage, we should not judge other believers for all moral things. There are other things we should not do, such as sin. The apostle John warns, "And now, little children, abide in Him, that when He appears, we may have confidence and not be ashamed before Him at His coming" (1 Jn. 2:28). The Judgment Seat of Christ is the final exam, what do we need to do now to pass the exam?

Do Everything as Unto the Lord

Paul tells slaves "whatever you do, do it heartily, as to the Lord and not to men" (Col. 3:23). All that a slave does, no job being left out, was to be done heartily, from the inside, as unto the Lord and not unto men.

A slave is to perform this kind of work "knowing that from the Lord you will receive the reward of the inheritance; for you serve the Lord Christ" (Col. 3:24a). In other words, God not only sees, but He also rewards the kind of work Paul is commanding. Slaves received no wages and had no legal right of inheritance. Paul informs them that if they do what they were forced to do anyway, *as unto the Lord*, they will receive a just and full reward from Him. The ancients considered slaves chattel. God treats believing, obedient slaves as heirs (Carson).

The inheritance is usually explained as heaven (Eadie), but if the inheritance is heaven, heaven is gained by works! The inheritance is a reward (see "reward consisting of inheritance" in the NASB margin; "an inheritance from the Lord as a reward" in the NIV; "inheritance as your reward" in the ESV; compensation "consisting of the inheritance" in JFB; "just recompense consisting in the inheritance" in the *Expositors Greek NT*; and "inheritance… as a reward" in the *Bible Knowledge Commentary*; see also Constable).

Dillow says, "The inheritance is a reward received as 'wages' for work done. Nothing could be plainer. The context is speaking of the return a man should receive because of his work, as in an employer-employee relationship. The inheritance is received as a result of work; it does not come as a gift. The Greek antapodosis means repayment or reward. The verb antapodidomi never means to receive as a gift; it is always used in the New Testament of a repayment due to an obligation" (Dillow, p. 68). God will reimburse believers at the Judgment Seat of Christ.

Paul explains, "For you serve the Lord Christ" (Col. 3:24b). The expression "the Lord Christ" only occurs here and in Romans 16:18. Thus, the Christian slave should work heartily for the Lord and not half-heartedly for people because God is the employer who will truly reimburse him. He will do that at the Judgment Seat of Christ. Salvation is "according to grace; judgment is according to works" (Bruce).

On the other hand, "He who does wrong will be repaid for the wrong which he has done; and there is no partiality" (Col. 3:25). The Greek word rendered "wrong" means "to do wrong, act wickedly, or criminally." The Greek word translated "repay" means "to receive back, recover" (*cf.* the English word "boomerang"). Christian slaves should not presume upon their position before God, thinking that God will overlook their misdeeds because they are mistreated or because they are Christians. There may have been a tendency for slaves to assume that because the favoritism of men was on the side of the master, there would be favoritism of God on the side of the slaves. That assumption is incorrect.

When he was a boy, Harry worked for a shoemaker and had to prepare leather for the soles of shoes. The piece of cowhide was first cut to size. Then, it was soaked in water and finally pounded with a flat-head hammer until it was hard and dry. It was a wearisome task and a tedious process Harry wished could be avoided. One day, he passed another shoe shop and paused to watch the shoe cobbler through the window. His boss's competitor did not pound the soles but took them from the water and nailed them immediately to the shoe. He approached the cobbler and said, "I noticed that you put the soles on while they are wet. Are they just as good as if they are pounded?" With a twinkle in his eye, the man replied, "No, but they come back much quicker that way, my boy."

Young Harry hurried back to his boss and suggested they were wasting time pounding and drying out the leather so carefully. His Christian employer read him Colossians 3:23 and explained that he did not cobble shoes just for the money, but he was doing it for the glory of God. He told Harry, "If I have to view every shoe I ever repaired at the Judgment Seat of Christ, I would dread to have the Lord say, 'Dan, that was a poor job; you didn't do your best.' Rather, I want to see His smile and hear His 'Well done, good and faithful servant.'" That young lad was Harry Ironside, who later became the pastor of the Moody Church in Chicago.

Practice Love and Mercy

Love John writes, "Love has been perfected among us in this: that we may have boldness in the day of judgment" (1 Jn. 4:17a). If we love others, His love has matured in us (1 Jn. 4:12). Someone has suggested that there are stages to love. In infancy, it is "I love me." As we grow, it is "I love me and thee (parents)—sometimes." When we get married, it is "I love you—if ...." The ultimate stage of love is simply, "I love you." There is a stage beyond that. It is to love others as believers and have God's love perfected in you. God loves us unconditionally. As we love others, we more fully apprehend and appreciate that reality.

When God's love is matured in us, we can be sure that we will have boldness before the Judgment Seat of Christ. The Greek word translated "confidence" in 1 John 2:28 is the same one rendered "boldness" in 1 John 4:17. It means "the freedom to speak, openness, boldness, confidence."

We can be sure we will have confidence before the Judgment Seat of Christ "because as He is, so are we in the world" (1 Jn. 4:17b). Confidence is predicated on our likeness to the Judge. The Judge is love (4:8). When we love, we are like Him.

Furthermore, John goes on to explain, "There is no fear in love; because perfect love casts out fear" (1 Jn. 4:18a). Love and fear are mutually exclusive (Plummer); they cannot coexist. They are as incompatible as oil and water (Stott). When God's love is matured by loving others, fear of meeting the Judge is cast out. As John further explains, "because fear involves torment" (1 Jn. 4:18b). The Greek word translated "torment" means "punishment." Unloving believers fear facing the Judge. They are in torment. They feel guilty and apprehensive. Fear carries with it a kind of torment that is its own punishment (Hodges).

Fear then contains that kind of torment and punishment, so John concludes, "but he who fears has not been made perfect in love" (1 Jn. 4:18c). Such fear indicates that the person who experiences it has not matured in love.

The point is that loving others gives us confidence before the Judgment Seat of Christ. Let me illustrate. Suppose there was a Latin test on Friday. The students would desperately walk around with a Latin book under their noses, conjugating verbs all week. They sleep verbs, talked verbs, and breathed verbs. Then, there was the girl walking across the campus with her tennis shoes on and a tennis racket in her hand. Someone says, "Where are you going? Don't you know that there is a Latin test on Friday?" "Yes," she replies. "Well, aren't you afraid you'll lose out if you don't study?" She might respond, "I know Latin. I've studied all through the term. I have it all, and I'm ready for the test." Since she had learned Latin, she had no fear. If we hadn't learned the lesson, we would be afraid. If we have loved others, there is no need for fear. We will have no fear at the Judgment Seat of Christ, provided we learned our lessons.

In singing the "Trust and Obey," a small boy in Sunday School misspoke. He sang, "Trust and okay."

Mercy James exhorts, "So speak and so do as those who will be judged by the law of liberty" (Jas. 2:12). In this passage, James teaches us that we should not practice prejudice (Jas. 2:1-11). He concludes that discussion by reminding his readers that what they say and do will be judged by the law of liberty, which is the law of love (Jas. 1:25). Laws usually limit. The law of love liberates.

Spiritual Basics: The Judgment Seat

James explains the judgment of verse 12 in verse 13 ("for"). "For judgment is without mercy to the one who has shown no mercy. Mercy triumphs over judgment" (Jas. 2:13). If believers are the type of people who have dispensed mercy during their lifetime, they will be judged mercifully at the Judgment Seat of Christ. If they have been harsh, unmerciful, and played favorites with people, they will not receive mercy at the Judgment Seat of Christ. The way believers treat others is the way God will treat them.

Summary: At the Judgment Seat of Christ, believers will give an account, be revealed, rewarded, and repaid.

On that blank page in the back of your Bible, under "Basics," write "12. The Judgmnet Seat," and after that, "2 Corinthians 5:10."

At the Judgment Seat of Christ, everything, including motives, will be evaluated (2 Cor. 5:10). Believers will give an account of all they do (Rom. 14:10). The two passages that mention the Judgment Seat of Christ by name (Rom. 14:10; 2 Cor. 5:10) combined with Colossians 3:25 indicate that at the Judgment Seat of Christ, believers will be rewarded for the good things they do in life, and will be repaid for the "bad/evil" (2 Cor. 5:10), "wrong" (Col. 3:25) things they have done. These verses raise questions about the nature of a reward and repayment, but they do not supply the answers. What is good? What is bad/evil? What is the reward? What is the repayment? I do not know all that is involved in this process because, as far as I can determine, the New Testament does not answer all the questions. Based on what I know, it seems that the New Testament is probably saying that all we do will be evaluated. Suppose you received As, Bs, and a few Fs in class. The final grade will consider all you did, the As and the Fs. That final grade would be a B.

Everything will be taken into consideration, and based on our final "grade," we will be rewarded. Perhaps the repayment it will be the shame (1 Jn. 2:28) and the torment (1 Jn. 4:18) of realizing just how much we have failed the Lord.

Some feel it is wrong for us to be motivated by the prospect of reward. Granted, because of what the Lord has done for us, we should be willing to serve Him with no thought of reward. Nevertheless, receiving rewards for serving the Lord is not our idea but His idea! So, something is wrong if we're not motivated by reward. To resist wanting rewards is pseudo-spirituality. It goes against the grain of the way the Lord tries to motivate us. Suppose a father told his son, "If you do the yard work Saturday, I'll pay you $25 and take you out to a nice dinner." Would it be wrong for the father to use those things to motivate his son? Would it be wrong for the son to be motivated by the dollars and dinner *with his father*?

John Calvin said, "It is my happiness that I have served Him who never fails to reward His servants to the full extent of His promise." John Bunyan said, "Whatever good thing you do for Him, if done according to the Word, is laid up for you a treasure in chests and coffers, to be brought out to be rewarded before both men and angels, to your eternal comfort."

Is it possible there will be levels of happiness in heaven? Some people can be happy living in a small house in a crowded neighborhood, but those living on a cliff overlooking the Pacific Ocean would have the joy the others did not have, although both would be happy.

Since everything you do will be judged at the Judgment Seat of Christ, do everything you do as unto the Lord and practice love and mercy. In ancient times, a sculptor was employed to construct a statue in a Greek temple. He meticulously and conscientiously made a beautiful and ornate statue, even the part against the wall. When asked why he carved the back with the same care as the front, he replied, "That's how I always work. Men may never see it, but I believe the gods do." He, of course, was mistaken about the gods, but the Christian slave who works with the same attitude about God is not.

CONCLUSION

In each chapter throughout the series, I have suggested that on a back page in the black of your Bible, you write the word "basics," and under that, write the topic and text for each of the 12 chapters.

1. Salvation	Ephesians 2:8-9
2. Assurance	John 3:36
3. Security	John 5:24
4. Trials	James 1:2-4
5. The Word	James 1:22
6. Understanding	Ephesians 5:17
7. Prayer	Matthew 7:7
8. Growth	2 Peter 3:18
9. Will of God	Romans 12:1-3
10. Provision of God	Philippians 4:19.
11. Love of God	Ephesians 3:17-18
12. Judgment Sest	2 Corinthians 5:10

The summary of the basic biblical spiritual truths people need to grow spiritually begins with establishing a secure relationship with Jesus Christ by trusting Him for the gift of eternal life. Believers are to handle trials with faith and endurance to grow to spiritual maturity. The initial relationship with the Lord develops into an intimate relationship with the Lord as believers understand, developing righteousness, love, and wisdom.

Additional basic biblical spiritual truths include: everything you need to know about the will of God is in the Word of God; God gives believers the freedom to make a number of life decisions, which should be made based on wisdom. At the same time, God wants His children to know He wants to be their God, providing for them as they cast all their care upon Him. He loves them with a sacrificial, everlasting love and rewards them for their faithful service.

These are the basic keys to spiritual growth, but they only work as you use them unlocked life and live a biblical spiritual life.

BIBLIOGRAPHY

Abbott-Smith. G., A Manuel Greek Lexicon of the New Testament. Edinburgh: T & T Clark, 1960 (reprint of the 1937 edition).

Barclay, William. *More New Testament Words*. London: SCM Press, 1958.

_____. *The Gospel of Matthew*, 2 vol. Philadelphia: The Westminster Press, 1958.

_____. *The Letter to the Philippians, Colossians, and Thessalonians*. Philadelphia: The Westminster Press, 1958.

Barnes, Albert. *Barnes' Notes*. www.e-sword.net

Berkhof, L. *Systematic Theology*. Grand Rapids: Wm. B. Eerdmans Publishing, 1961.

Bruce, F. F. *The Epistles to the Colossians, to Philemon and to the Ephesians*, New International Commentary on the New Testament, Grand Rapids: Wm. B. Eerdmans Publishing Co., 1968.

Bromiley, G. W. " Faith," *The International Standard Bible Encyclopedia*, vol. II, Grand Rapids: William B Eerdmans and Publishing Company, 1982

Clarke, Adam. *Adam Clarke's Commentary on the Bible*. E-sword.net.

Cocoris, G. Michael. *Evangelism: A Biblical Approach*. Chicago: Moody Press, 1984.

Constable, Thomas L. *Constable's Notes*. www.soniclight.com/constable/notes.htm.

Cranfield, C. E. B. *A Critical and Exegetical Commentary on the Epistle to the Romans*. International Critical Commentary series. 2 vols. Edinburgh: T. & T. Clark, 1975.

Dillow, Joseph C. *The Reign of the Servant Kings*. Miami Springs, Fla.: Schoettle Publishing Co., 1992.

Eadie, John. *Commentary on the Epistle to the Colossians*. Grand Rapids: Zondervan Publishing House, 1957.

Expositors Greek New Testament. Bible Analyzer 4 Software, 2012.

Friesen, Garry. *Decision Making and the Will of God: A Biblical Alternative to the Traditional View*. Sisters, OR: Multnomah Press, 1980.

Geisler, Norman L. "Colossians," *The Bible Knowledge Commentary, New Testament*, edited by John Walvoord and Roy B. Zuck. Wheaton, IL: Victor books, 1983.

Gingrich, F. Wilbur and Frederick W. Danker, eds. *A Greek-English Lexicon of the New Testament and Other Early Christian Literature*, 2nd ed. Chicago: The University of Chicago Press, 1979.

Hansel, Tim. *Holy Sweat*. Waco, TX, Word Books Publisher, 1987.

Hodges, Zane C. *Absolutely Free*. Grand Rapids: Zondervan Publishing House, 1989.

_____ *The Epistle of James*. Irving, Texas: Grace Evangelical Society, 1994.

Hoehner, Harold W. "Ephesians" in *The Bible Knowledge Commentary: New Testament*, Edited by John F. Walvoord and Roy B. Zuck. Wheaton: Scripture Press Publications, Victor Books, 1983.

Hubbard, Jr., Robert L. *The Book of Ruth* (The New International Commentary on the Old Testament). Grand Rapids: Wm. B. Eerdmans Publishing Company, 1988.

Ironside, H. A. *Full Assurance*. Chicago: Moody Press, 1937.

Jamieson, Robert, A. R. Fausset, David Brown. *Jamieson, Fausset, and Brown's Commentary on the Whole Bible*. www.e-sword.net

Johnston, J. K. *Why Christians Sin*. Grand Rapids, MI. Discovery House, 1992.

Kidner, Derek. *Psalms*. Tyndale Old Testament Commentaries series. Leicester and Downers Grove, Ill.: InterVarsity Press, 1973.

MacDonald, William. *The Bible Believer's Commentary*, edited by Arthur Farstad, Nashville: Thomas Nelson Publishers, 1989, the e-sword edition.

Mayor, Joseph. *The Epistle of St. James*. Grand Rapids: Zondervan Publishing House, 1954.

Mitton, C. Leslie. *The Epistle of James*. Grand Rapids: Wm. B. Eerdmans Publishing Co., 1966.

Machen, Gresham J. *What is Faith?* Grand Rapids: Wm. B. Eerdmans Publishing Co., 1965.

Morris, Leon. *Ruth, an Introduction and Commentary*. Leicester: Inter-Varsity Press, 1968.

_____. *The Gospel According to John*. The New International Commentary on the New Testament. Grand Rapids: William B. Eerdmans Publishing Company, 1984.

Rice, John R. *Prayer: Asking and Receiving*. Murfreesboro, TN: Sword of the Lord Publications, 1970.

Ryrie, Charles Caldwell. *So Great Salvation*. Wheaton: Scripture Press Publications, Victor Books, 1989.

_____. *The Ryrie Study Bible*. Chicago: Moody Press, 1978.

Schaeffer, Francis. *How Shall We Then Live?* Grands Rapids: Fleming H. Revell Company, 1975

Tenney, Merrill C., *John: The Gospel of Belief*. Grand Rapids: William B. Eerdmans, 1960.

The NKJV Study Bible. Edited by Earl D. Radmacher. Nashville: Thomas Nelson Publishers, 1997.

Vaughan, Curtis. *Colossians: A Study Guide Commentary*. Grand Rapids, Zondervan Publishing House, 1973.

About The Author

G. Michael Cocoris is a gifted communicator. He can make even complicated subjects simple, clear, and practical. His breadth of experience has allowed him to relate to a wide range of audiences.

Michael received a Bachelor of Arts degree from Tennessee Temple University, a Master of Theology degree from Dallas Seminary, and a Doctorate of Divinity from Biola University. He traveled the United States for over a dozen years as a speaker. He has also been a seminary professor, visiting lecturer, and world traveler, including hosting tours to Israel and China.

Michael has pastored three churches, including a rural church when he was in seminary, an urban church, the historic Church of the Open Door, first in downtown Los Angeles and later in Glendora, California, and a suburban church, the Lindley Church in Tarzana California, a suburb of Los Angeles. While at the Church of Open Door, he had a daily radio broadcast.

Michael has written numerous magazine articles, mainly for Biblical Research Monthly. He has authored a number of books, including *Seventy Years on Hope Street, A History of the Church of the Open Door; The Spiritual Life, Clarifying the Confusion; Repentance, The Most Misunderstood Word in the Bible; Evangelism: A Biblical Approach; The Salvation Controversy; Lordship Salvation: Is It Biblical?; The Books of the Bible, the Subject, Structure, Situation, and Significant Verses of Each Book; Psalms, A Song for Every Situation, Each Summarized on One Page; Counseling Theories: A Simple Explanation and Biblical Evaluation; Proverbs; Autopsy of the United States; How to Study the Bible; and Spiritual Basics, Basic Biblical Keys to Living a Spiritual Life.* In addition, he was a contributor to The NKJV Study Bible and *Nelson's New Illustrated Bible Commentary.*

Michael is the pastor of the Lindley Church in Tarzana, California. He and his wife, Patricia, live in Santa Monica, California.

www.ingramcontent.com/pod-product-compliance
Lightning Source LLC
Chambersburg PA
CBHW070058080526
44586CB00013B/1112